humoR
for a
boomer's heart

Stories, Quips, and Quotes to Lift the Heart

humor
for a
boomer's heart

Compiled by Snapdragon Group℠ Editorial Services

Illustrated by Dennis Hill

HOWARD BOOKS
A DIVISION OF SIMON & SCHUSTER
New York   London   Toronto   Sydney

Patsy Clairmont, Anita Renfroe, Martha Bolton,
Brad Dickson, Charlene Baumbich, and many more

Our purpose at Howard Books is to:
- *Increase faith* in the hearts of growing Christians
- *Inspire holiness* in the lives of believers
- *Instill hope* in the hearts of struggling people everywhere

Because He's coming again!

 Howard Books, a division of Simon & Schuster, Inc.
1230 Avenue of the Americas, New York, NY 10020
www.howardpublishing.com

Humor for a Boomer's Heart © 2008 by Howard Books

Library of Congress Cataloging-in-Publication Data
Humor for a Boomer's Heart: stories, quips and quotes to lift the heart / compiled by Snapdragon Group[SM]; illustrated by Dennis Hill.
    p.cm.—(Humor for the heart)
    Summary: "Collection of original and previously published humorous stories about and for baby-boomers"—Provided by publisher.
    Includes bibliographical references.
    1. Baby-boomer's—Humor. I. Snapdragon Group[SM]

ISBN-13: 978-1-4165-7908-3
ISBN-10:   1-4165-7908-7

10 9 8 7 6 5 4 3 2 1

HOWARD colophon is a registered trademark of Simon & Schuster, Inc.

Manufactured in the United States

For information regarding special discounts for bulk purchases, please contact: Simon & Schuster Special Sales at 1-800-456-6798 or business@simonandschuster.com.

Manuscript compiled by Snapdragon Group[SM] Tulsa, Oklahoma, USA.
Illustrations by Dennis Hill
Interior Design by Masterpeace Studiology

Contents

Chapter 1: Play It Again, Sam (Boomer Culture)

Chapter 2: That Person in the Mirror Can't Be Me! (Beauty and Fitness)

Chapter 3: For Better or for Worse (Marriage)

Chapter 4: The Perilous View from the Top (Perspective on Life)

Chapter 5: Who Are These People? (Children)

Chapter 6: Who's Watching Mom and Dad? (Aging Parents)

Chapter 7: Embracing Bingo! (Aging and Health)

Chapter 8: Great Goobers! We have Grandchildren (Grandchildren)

Chapter 9: Rest and Riches (Retirement)

Chapter 10: Tales of the Open Road (Adventure)

Contributors—202

Source Notes—209

Chapter 1

Play It Again, Sam
(Boomer Culture)

Remember When...

- All soft drinks came in bottles.
- Cars had no air-conditioning.
- You got your windshield cleaned, oil checked, and gas pumped, without asking, all free, every time.
- Music was on vinyl records; singles were 45 rpm and albums were 33 ⅓ rpm.
- There was one light (red) on top of police cars.
- You could see a live Jan & Dean concert for $3.00.
- Gas was twenty-six cents a gallon and ethyl was way too high at thirty cents.
- Typing class was noisy.
- Cracker Jack had a decent, unusual prize in it.
- Every one you knew had a vaccination scar.
- You believed everything the government said.
- Every house had a tall outside TV antenna.
- Atomic war was a real everyday thought.
- Nobody owned a purebred dog.
- A quarter was a decent allowance, and another quarter was a huge bonus.
- The worst thing you could do at school was smoke in the bathrooms, flunk a test, or chew gum.
- A '55 Chevy was everyone's dream car—to cruise, peel out, or lay rubber.
- People went steady, and girls wore a class ring wrapped with an inch of yarn so it would fit their fingers.
- Decisions were made by chanting "eeny-meeny-miney-mo."

Therapeutic Theme Songs
Karen Scalf Linamen

Love can give your heart wings. It can also give you heartburn. My friend Diane was closer to the heartburn stage as she sat at my kitchen table and spilled her tale of woe.

She was dating a man who was madly in love with her and often talked about their future together. And she was in love with him, too. There was just one small problem.

"So why hasn't he proposed?" Diane whined.

I had no answers. What I did have was a bag of Oreo cookies, which, of course, is the next best thing.

Diane and I talked about her dilemma while eating the middles out of our cookies. We rehashed how they had met and how long they'd been together. We analyzed their educations, careers, families of origin—anything that could possibly have a bearing on Hector's debilitating proposal-phobia. And then, an

hour or so into our pity party, we made the Discovery. It changed everything. It gave us new perspective. It brought sanity and sense to the situation. Suddenly, life was grand.

It started when one of us—I don't remember who—looked thoughtfully into the distance and said, "Bet you can't sing all three stanzas of *The Brady Bunch* theme song."

Maybe it was the lateness of the hour. Maybe we had run out of things to analyze and were ready to tackle a challenge we actually had a shot at solving. Or maybe we'd just had too much chocolate.

Whatever the reason, Diane sang out, "Here's the story of a lovely lady . . ."

And I chimed in, "Who was bringing up three very lovely girls . . ."

"All of them had hair of gold, like their mother . . ."

"The youngest one in curls . . ."

Before we knew it, we had serenaded our way through the courtship of Mike and Carol Brady, belted out the theme to *The Beverly Hillbillies,* galloped through the *Mr. Ed* song, stumbled through an energetic rendition of all eight verses of *Gilligan's Island,* and sung several stanzas of "Doot, doot, doodoot doodoot doot," which any self-respecting baby boomer will recognize as the theme song to *I Dream of Jeannie.*

By this time, we were no longer concerned by the length of time it was taking Hector to propose, nor whether Diane and Hector's first home together would be a condo at Retirement World. No, our bigger concern at that moment had to do with the amount of money it must have taken to get Robert Reed to consent to that awful perm, and whether or not Ginger and the Professor were secretly in love with each other.

Since then, I've done a lot of thinking about the therapeutic power of TV theme songs.

There's no denying that belting out any song that begins "Green Acres is the place for me . . ." will leave us feeling lighter and brighter. And that road rage could be eradicated if we required angry drivers to sing a single stanza from "Gilligan's Island" before cutting someone off in traffic, flashing the finger, or cocking a handgun. And that when it comes to ulcers and other stress-induced maladies, a simple group sing-along of the theme from *The Monkees* can lower the blood pressure of folks with even the most extreme type-A tendencies.

Road rage could be eradicated if we required angry drivers to sing a single stanza from Gilligan's Island.

So why aren't more people tuning in to the benefits of baby boomer TV theme song therapy? I'm not sure, especially since a steady stream of this stuff could brighten anyone's day and wouldn't be all that difficult to arrange. Imagine replacing all the Barry Manilow muzak in elevators across the nation with the lively, pungent chords from *Sanford and Son* or the whistled strains from *The Andy Griffith Show*. And what customer service representative wouldn't prefer to answer a call from a holding customer who had just spent the last seventeen minutes listening to the *I Love Lucy* theme?

I'm telling you, simple steps like this could re-civilize our entire society. I'm not saying that listening to TV-Land theme songs will give you whiter teeth, a smaller waistline, and more money in the bank; but I'm not saying it won't.

Three weeks after my Oreo sing-along with Diane, Hector popped the question. He claims he'd been planning to propose for months, but I'm not convinced. All I know is that Diane and I sang TV theme songs . . . and Hector proposed. You can't tell me that was just a coincidence. There's a connection somehow.

Is there anything that TV-Land theme songs can't accomplish?

If you think of something, let me know. Call my cell phone. In fact, call my cell phone even if you can't think of something. I could use the lift.

My ringtone is the theme from *Taxi*.

10 Memorable Pairs of Pants
Bill Gray

1. DOUBLE-KNEE JEANS, 1959. Apparently, in addition to being short, having a Ringo-sized nose, and wearing a face that is not quite symmetrical, I have another physical cross to bear: My knees are too high.

When I was in elementary school, my jeans were expected to last the school year. This expectation meant nothing to my knees, which kept on making holes in the front of my jeans whenever I dropped and slid during an especially spirited game of girls catch the boys.

My mom, ever on the lookout to save money and avoid having to use upper-body strength to push a needle through denim, bought me a pair of double-knee jeans.

My knees refused to get out of joint over this. Instead, they came through the fabric just above the patch that had been glued to the inside of the pants legs to make the double knee.

After that, the double knees were mostly good for making it appear that I was smuggling cardboard beer coasters in my pants.

2. YELLOW CHECKED SLACKS, 1966. Desperate to appear mod, I purchased a pair of pants with small, windowpane checks all over them—in yellow.

They looked very cool, even though they were a bit snug. They were just barely wider around the cuff than my side-zipper

Desperate to appear mod, I purchased a pair of pants with small, windowpane checks all over them—in yellow.

Beatles boots, which meant I was constantly bending down to place the pants over the boots where they belonged. That Sheriff Taylor "pants tucked inside the boots" look was not for the in crowd, which I hoped I was in with.

The pants remained a bit snug until they were laundered, which caused them to shrink a size and a half. Defying all laws of physics, the pants actually became tighter than my skin. It was difficult to follow the junior high edict that shirts must always be tucked in. There wasn't enough waist room.

3. CORDUROY BELL-BOTTOMS, 1967. Bell-bottoms became fashionable long before it was possible to buy them at any store within driving distance. I wanted a pair, of course, and my salvation came in the form of a guy named Jim, who transferred to my little town's junior high from the mysterious big city.

Jim had long red hair, parted close to the center. So I liked

him right off. He also had a great pair of royal blue corduroy bell-bottoms.

Jim had a lot of cool clothes and, apparently, the money to buy more. He would grow tired of some of them and sell them to me. He sold me a World War I–style doughboy jacket with a stand-up collar and brass buttons. I wore it to school my first day of tenth grade, even though the coat was made of thick wool and the temperature was in the eighties.

But before that, he sold me the blue bell-bottoms. I was considering using that five-dollar bill to buy the Moby Grape album, but the blue bells seemed a wiser investment. And that was in spite of the fact that the album came with a big poster where one of the band members had managed to sneak an extended middle finger past the photographer.

I fairly glided down the halls with the pants on the next day, and when a friend of mine saw me, he said, "You're kidding, Gray . . . bell-bottoms?"

My choice was validated.

4. STRIPED PANTS, 1968. The ironies of life can sometimes be a big pain in the yin-yang.

I had been envying the really good local garage bands for a couple of years when I finally got asked to be in one. Of course, this had to come immediately after the new warden took charge of my high school. To keep from being kicked out, I had traded in my hard-earned Beatles hairstyle for a cut that was the only thing about me that resembled a Marine.

I would have to find some other way to be cool at the first gig with the new band, and I would have to find it yesterday.

Big-city Jim came to the rescue again. Turns out he had purchased my bell-bottoms from a catalog.

From the same catalog, I ordered a pair of pale blue jeans with inch-wide rust vertical stripes. The thin, muscular model in the catalog looked magnetic in them, and I assumed I would as well.

I dressed for the performance at the guitarist's house, and when I made my entrance down the stairs wearing the pants and a purple satin shirt with ruffled cuffs that I had also ordered, I could tell everyone was impressed. Or stunned. Or something.

5. PERFECT JEANS, 1968. Fortunately, stores where I lived began stocking bell-bottom jeans. Unfortunately, they were the Sonny-and-Cher kind, straight to about mid-ankle, then flared sharply at the bottom. They were better, but they weren't quite hip.

From my friend Truman, who was cool as a snow cone and knew these things, I learned where to get the right kind.

The legs on the pair I got were tight to the knees, then began a slow flaring triangle that widened until they dragged on the floor, leaving only the toes of my shoes visible.

These pants existed long, long ago, before the days of stone-washed or prewashed or acid-washed jeans. Blue jeans would start dark blue in those days, then fade incrementally over time and washings until, one day, you would put them on, and they would be perfect.

Those bells reached that stage, then just kept getting better. I wore them until they fell apart.

6. GRADUATION PANTS, 1970. I was a jeans and corduroy guy. Dress pants were for straights, which meant something different in those days.

So when high school graduation time finally crawled around, my mom had to buy me a pair of dress pants. They were black, with creases so sharp I could have shaved with them, on the one day a week I had to shave.

They were 29/32s, snug around the waist, and plenty long enough to wear with the stacked-heel suede cowboy boots I wore to my commencement.

I kept those pants for ten years after graduation and never wore them. Once a year I took them out of the closet and tried them on to see if they still fit. One year they didn't. That's the year I finally gave them away.

7. PATCHED STRAIGHT LEGS, 1973. I don't know quite when it started. Some rock star, I suppose, showed up with a patch on his blue jeans. Pretty soon everybody who wasn't nobody started patching his or her jeans until it became a contest to see who would have the most interesting patches.

The rules were simple: You could patch with anything except blue denim.

My straight legs actually did wear through in a knee, so I patched it. That was cool, so I patched the other knee because it looked like it might wear through soon. After that I became a patcher without a cause. Red squares, green circles, plaid material from an old work shirt, corduroy, burlap, flannel.

I covered the hole in the back, where the corner of the pocket tore off, with a peace symbol. The long, thin, "U.S. Army" iron-on from an army shirt worked fine for the inside seam. An American flag went behind the hole in the crotch so the stripes showed through the frayed fabric.

I was actually relieved to finally throw those pants away.

Sewing is hard. I could see why my mom went with the double knees.

8. WHITE PLEATED WALKING SHORTS, 1980. I didn't wear shorts in the 1960s. We wore long jeans in the hottest weather. We didn't mind being hot, as long as we were cool.

The old jeans we had cut off were saved primarily for swimming. Even then we would, often as not, just swim in our jeans and then walk them dry again.

So it was quite a lifestyle-changing experience for me to wear the white pleated walking shorts.

It was right after I got engaged, and I really wanted to impress my future in-laws. I figured the shorts oughta do it. Just in case, I also shaved off the straggly beard and traded in my round-rimmed Lennon glasses for a pair of grown-up frames.

It's twenty-some years later, and I'm still married to their daughter.

Some guys slay two-headed, fire-breathing dragons for love. I change my pants.

9. DOCKERS, 1983. I don't know. The date is hazy. It was some time around '83, I think.

It had been jeans—blue or black—for me since, well, forever. When I needed to get dressed up, I wore corduroy. Except for graduations, funerals, and my wedding, that was as far as I went toward the dark side.

Pleated, cuffed khakis had always been around, but to middle-aged hippies like me, they were out of the question. Weak tea, I thought. Chess club. College fraternities. The Lettermen. Neither

fish nor fowl. You think you're cool in those things just because they're not actually, technically, dress pants. Right? Think again, nerd-o.

So it came as quite a little shock to me when I tried a pair on and caught myself thinking that they looked pretty good. And felt even better.

I had met the enemy and was wearing his pants.

10. CORDUROY PAINTER'S PANTS, 2001. I buy most of my clothes on the cheap now, cruising the sale racks like a tiger shark through a school of tuna.

Fashion has become less of an issue to me, for one thing. And since I can clearly remember when you could buy jeans and get change from a ten, I recoil at sixty-dollar pants. The sight of a guy my age recoiling is not pretty.

I had met the enemy and was wearing his pants.

I was looking through the 70-percent-off rack when I spotted two pairs of corduroy painter's pants, one tan and one olive. They were both in my size, which is to say loose around the middle and just a little too long

I held them at arm's length for a long while, these fancy britches that looked like work pants, but would never feel the worn leather of a tool belt.

These were young-guy pants. No doubt about that.

I put them back.

I took them off the rack again.

I put them back again.

Finally, I bought them.

I know that they were already out of style when I bought them, or they wouldn't have been 70 percent off. I know I look a little goofy, swoosh-swoosh-swooshing around with the baggy legs flapping and bunching up on my shoes.

They remind me of my youth.

You want better than that from a pair of pants?

Turn On, Tune In, Drop Everything
Bill Gray

Much has been made of the fact that mine is the first generation to have grown up with TV. Psychologists, preachers, principals, and probably some other p-words have told us how we're all being sucked into a cesspool of moral ruination at warp speed by the unholy eye in the living room. It's the devil in living color, they say. It's chewing gum for the mind. It's a waste of time.

Ahhh, so's yer old man.

Look at me. I've been watching TV my whole life, and I'm perfectly norm—well, OK, bad example.

I suppose there was no TV in my house when I was born in 1952, but there was one there as far back as I can remember. One of my favorite childhood memories, in fact, is coming home from school, grabbing a fistful of Hydrox cookies and a glass of milk for dunkin', then falling to the linoleum in front of Roy Rogers.

To my way of thinking, Roy and Dale and Gabby were at

least as educational as school was. From Roy I learned always to shoot to wing, never to kill. From Gabby I learned the value of good dental hygiene. And who knew there were Jeeps in the "old West?"

We've all been entertained by television. But even beyond that, TV has given us something to talk about. And as anyone who's ever been to a company picnic knows, that's a valuable gift.

Someday, if I don't face early cancellation from that great programmer in the sky, I expect to be discussing TV shows down at the senior center.

In high school, you bet your bippy we all started saying "Sock it to me!" when *Laugh-In* debuted. And we kept using the show's catch phrases, too, right up to the time teachers started saying them.

Contrary to those who said TV would turn our brains to oatmeal, TV has been *berra berra* good to me.

Of course, there were others, and there still are shows that affect us like that. More than entertainment, they tint our culture, enter our vocabularies, change the way we dress or wear our hair.

Admit it. You wore the suit coat over the T-shirt. You asked the stylist to cut your hair like Farrah's. You lusted after Michael's leather bomber jacket. OK, maybe that last one was just me.

Don't have a cow about it, man.

I have to agree, though, that a lot of television over the years has been mindless drivel. That's not necessarily a bad thing.

Sometimes after a hard day at life, the spirit prefers nachos to carrot sticks.

But I also know that in the forty-five years or so I've been watching TV, there has been at least one show every season that I just can't wait to see.

Sometimes they've been the big hits, like *M*A*S*H* or *Hill Street Blues*. Sometimes they've been the ones that don't last long, like *He and She* or *Sports Night*. But they've always been there, impressing me with great writing and innovative styles.

Indeed, contrary to those who said TV would turn our brains to oatmeal, TV has been *berra berra* good to me. Turns out, while I was collecting all that TV trivia in the brain drawers where geography and math should have been, I was actually preparing for my future job. I learned more about writing jokes from TV than from any textbook, and I've made good use of lots of TV references in the greeting cards I write. The same is true of every other humor writer at Hallmark.

Of course, like everything else, my viewing habits have changed over the years.

I no longer watch a lot of TV, in spite of what you might hear from some people who shall remain my wife. There have been many evenings in my past when I turned the TV on at 6:30 and turned it off on my way to bed. I don't do that anymore. I mean, that would be almost three hours.

Instead, I usually watch only the shows I can't wait to see. And I usually watch those on tape sometime after they've run. Last season there were three of them, all hour-long dramas.

This is an ironic thing. When I was a kid, we had two channels with "sort of OK" reception. We could just barely make out

17

the very snowy picture on a third channel, but only if one of us was on the roof holding the antenna aloft in the night sky.

Now we have cable, which is to say we are air-breathing mammals in suburbia. I have many channels I never watch. Two sports channels. Not interested in sports. Two hip-hop channels. See: sports. We have cable mostly for CNN, the clear picture, and the cartoons.

But I still love TV. I'm still amazed that it's right there, and I can watch it when I feel like it. TV is an old friend I haven't lost touch with over the years.

I can't wait to see what the next great show will be.

Time Travel in the Sixties
Vicki J. Kuyper

I was a flower child caught in a time warp. For the first thirteen years of my life, California's San Francisco Bay area was home . . . birthplace to the Beat generation, haven for the great unwashed, a hotbed of hippie unrest. I loved it. Almost every weekend, my family would drive to the Haight-Ashbury district across the bay and gawk at the flower children. And even though I was barely on the brink of adolescence, I fancied myself one of them.

In elementary school, I joined a band. I couldn't play an instrument or sing, but man, could I dance. That's how I became the one and only official go-go dancer for the Psychedelic Pineapple. We only knew one song, "Satisfaction" by the Rolling Stones. Of course, at the age of nine I didn't have a clue as to what we were singing about, but once that electric guitar riff started, I did the Swim and the Jerk like the Energizer bunny on speed.

Then we moved to Santa Rosa. Only one hour north of

San Francisco, it felt like it was the far side of the moon. Here families spent their weekends entering pie competitions at county fairs, skating at the Charles Schulz Ice Arena, or strolling through the well-manicured Luther Burbank Gardens. To me, the only thing Santa Rosa seemed to be a hotbed of was boredom.

Though I had to admit, it was a step above option number two, which was moving to the nearby city of Petaluma. Petaluma wasn't any less groovy than Santa Rosa, as if that were even possible. But my father's plan was to move his company into a business park by the railroad tracks—and our family with it. We toured the nearly empty warehouse, where plastic partitions marked off cubicles on the beige linoleum floor. The heels of my go-go boots echoed against the high, recessed ceilings, where pipes of every description zigzagged above my head in full view. I pictured my bed in a cubicle . . . showering in the company washroom . . . inviting friends over to the business park for a slumber party. Even though I was too young to know about zoning laws, I was pretty sure the school bus wasn't going to stop here.

At least in Santa Rosa we'd have an actual house. And soon, that house would be filled with new friends. At least, that's the way I pictured it. In preparation for making all these newfound friends, I donned my favorite outfit for the first day of school. From the tip of my white, patent leather go-go boots to the top of my head of long, straight, red hair, I was a poster child for the sixties that morning. My neon, psychedelic print mini-dress, with its lace-embellished muttonchop sleeves, coordinated perfectly with my antacid pink fishnets. (I loved the way those fishnets left my thighs looking like an underdone waffle for hours after I'd removed them!) A homemade leather choker, with a fake-gold peace symbol glued onto it, completed my ensemble.

20

After finishing up paperwork in the principal's office, a school secretary walked me, in all my go-go booted glory, to my first class of the day. As she opened the classroom door, I readied myself with a warm smile. "This is Vicki Miller," she announced, "a new student here at Rincon Valley Jr. High."

Although I don't think there was an actual, audible, collective gasp, the look on my future classmates' faces told the whole story. Well, most of the story. The rest of it was told by what they were wearing. The guys were clad in dress pants with plaid or striped button-down shirts. Not a hair on their heads was long enough to touch their neatly pressed collars. And as for the girls, they wore wool skirts, mostly plaid, with turtlenecks, knee-high stockings, and penny loafers, their finger-waved hair held back with plastic barrettes. Talk about a time warp.

This flower child broke the first rule of hippiedom. She chose to conform.

I spent the rest of the day feeling like a clown who'd accidentally joined a funeral procession. I tried to smile, but my self-confidence had plummeted to record lows. That night, I put my favorite dress in the back of the closet and never took it out again. This flower child broke the first rule of hippiedom. She chose to conform.

Eventually I did make friends in Santa Rosa. Great friends. I even learned to enjoy the benefits of small-town living. And at my thirty-year high school reunion, I had the pleasure of reconnecting with some of those same classmates from Rincon Valley Jr. High. As we parted that night, one of them whispered, "I'll never forget what you wore to school that first day!" Neither will I.

Angus MacGyver and Other Long-lost Loves

Karen Scalf Linamen

Raise your hand if you used to have a crush on MacGyver. In case you've been living on another planet for the past twenty years, Richard Dean Anderson created the television character of secret agent Angus MacGyver (yes, *Angus*) in the eighties. If you watched the show, the first things you noticed about the character were his boyish smile and great hair. After that, it might dawn on you that he also had a knack for using common household items to get himself out of life-threatening jams. In fact, the climax of every show involved watching MacGyver survive situations such as being trapped in a room with a ticking bomb with nothing on hand to save himself except, oh, I don't know, some dryer lint and a Bic pen.

OK, I made up the part about the dryer lint. But the real story lines didn't sound any more plausible (although part of the fun of the show was that MacGyver's inventions were scientifically possible, even if they weren't very probable).

For example, in one episode he had to destroy a laser. Thank goodness he had cigarettes and binoculars on hand!

He plugged a sulfuric acid leak with chocolate.

He repaired a blown fuse using an aluminum gum wrapper.

He smashed through a door (and took out two armed guards) using a slingshot made from bed springs.

He built a bomb out of a fire extinguisher. He recharged a battery with wine. He fixed a broken fuel line with a ballpoint pen. And when his getaway car had a broken radiator, all he could find to save himself were egg whites, but—wouldn't you know it?—that was exactly what he needed to do the job.

But back to the crush thing.

I'm not *advocating* having crushes on fictional TV characters, or even on celebrities. For one thing, those kinds of relationships can feel one-sided because fictional characters and celebrities rarely return phone calls. The best you can hope for is that, after placing hundreds of phone calls, you might get a response in the form of a restraining order. So you can see that, for the amount of effort you have to expend in order to get any kind of response at all, you really are better off owning a fish.

Nevertheless, we've all done the celebrity crush thing. And not just women, either. Guys have crushes, too.

Last week I attended a banquet for couples and singles in their forties and above. At my table, eight acquaintances chatted politely about their careers, the ages of their children, the rising price of gas, and the health of the economy. It was all very

grown-up and sedate and, eventually, I couldn't stand it one more minute.

I looked at the man across the table from me and said very seriously, "Dave, I have a very important question for you."

He said, "Sure."

I said, "Your answer may reveal more about you than you may intend, but I encourage you to consider your words carefully, and to be as honest as possible. Are you ready?"

By now we had the attention of everyone at our table.

Dave sat up a little straighter and squared his jaw. I sensed he was as ready as he'd ever be.

I posed my question.

"Ginger or Mary Ann?"

I wish I could adequately describe what happened next. Turns out, among the men at our table, three'd had crushes on Mary Ann and one still carried a torch for Mrs. Howell. When the choice was between Jan and Marsha, I thought we'd have an even split until one man opted out and voted for Emma Peel of the *Avengers*. When someone brought up police women and the choice came down to Angie Dickinson or Sharon Gless as Chris Cagney, the boys at our table scoffed and said no contest: Angie won hands down.

Dave sat up a little straighter and squared his jaw. I sensed he was as ready as he'd ever be.

By now, there wasn't a single grown-up at our table. Oh, to the casual observer I imagine we still looked like men and women approaching fifty. But I knew

differently. I knew that, at least for a moment, the year was 1969, and we were all in the throes of our first adolescent crushes.

For the rest of the evening, the memories and laughter flowed freely, and by the time we parted ways, there were promises to get together again, perhaps at someone's home, maybe for dinner, maybe to watch *The Wizard of Oz* with the sound off and Pink Floyd on the stereo.

We'd come a long way from casual acquaintances making grown-up small talk.

And that's a feat even MacGyver could appreciate.

He was an old man who fished alone in...

Speed Reader on Board

Marti Attoun

My husband questioned my financial savvy the other night as I drove across town on gas that cost $2.94 a gallon to buy a Jiffy cornbread mix on sale three for a dollar.

"It'd be cheaper to grow our own corn and hire someone to grind it," he said.

I didn't dare confess the true reason for my dash across town. I'd bought an old Carl Hiassen audiobook for a buck at a garage sale and had reached a cliffhanger. The Orange Bowl queen was in grave danger of being blown off her float. I couldn't wait another mile. I needed an excuse to drive—now.

While we all fret about fuel prices jacking up the cost of our hauled goods—from avocados to airline tickets—no one seems alarmed about the hit to literacy. With these ridiculous gas prices, audio-bookworms can't afford to read.

For example, two dollars' worth of gas used to get me through two

chapters in my thrifty Toyota. Even if the prose is pruned to short verbs and the narrator is a quick-tongued Easterner instead of a Southerner with an accent as thick as motor oil, I'm feeling the crunch.

I could take my audiobook indoors, obviously, and listen while idling on the couch. But for me that would defeat the purpose and pleasure of audiobooks. I like the multitasking aspect—"reading" on my way to the dentist's office, while punching in my PIN number at the ATM, or waiting in the drive-through lane to place my sausage and biscuit order.

Hitting the open road with an open book feels oh-so-breezy; continuing one's education while continuing down the highway behind a Wal-Mart semi is the American way.

Continuing my education while continuing down the highway behind a Wal-Mart semi is the American way.

For the longest time, I was an audiobook snob, though—sailing past the three aisles of recorded books at our local library. Surely, I thought, listening to Hemingway at seventy miles per hour couldn't be considered real reading.

Now I'm convinced that *The Old Man and the Sea* is best read at seventy miles per hour; seventy-five might actually be better. I checked out the classic, which I'd managed to dodge in high school, and read it on a solo business trip from my driveway in the Missouri Ozarks to Colorado.

Before I'd reached Hays, Kansas, old Santiago's marlin had been picked clean by sharks. I, too, felt gutted, but was bone happy. One literary landscape behind me, miles and miles of classics to go.

Since then, my car has become a bookmobile of sorts, and I no longer stew about bumper-to-bumper traffic or road-construction

slowdowns while the plot thickens and the protagonist finds a detour around life's snarls.

As other drivers do, I have an occasional outburst, but it's only because that spineless David in *The Memory Keeper's Daughter* can't summon the wherewithal to tell his sweet wife that he gave away their daughter.

Exorbitant gasoline prices, though, are putting the skids on my reading. I've tried listening to the abridged—and thus more fuel-efficient—audiobooks, but that's like driving solely on the Interstate and missing all the stranger-than-fiction scenes and characters along the country roads and town squares—the chain-saw artist who carves giant wooden buzzards and sells them from his front yard, and Sid's Diner, which serves hamburgers in hubcaps.

I've tried car-pooling and listening to audiobooks at the same time, but that's next to impossible unless all the passengers are in the same audiobook club. I have discovered that even family members who are passengers in the car can be a roadblock for an audiobook-lover.

Last Saturday, for example, I volunteered to drive my car on the garage-sale circuit with my husband because I was itching to get going on the mystery that I'd just checked out.

"Sue Grafton will be joining us," I said. "I hope you don't mind."

"Who?" he asked. "She isn't that flake in your clogging class who collects old tap shoes, is she?"

I just sighed, turned the key in the ignition, and switched on National Public Radio.

"No," I told him. "You're thinking of Willa Cather."

Mark my words. If gas prices keep skyrocketing, we're going to be a nation of illiterates.

Already, some of us wouldn't recognize a good plot-driven book if it ran over us.

Fifty-nine-and-three-quarters
Dixon Hearne

That '70s Show has done as much to confound as to enlighten younger audiences. My granddaughter, Ashley, who lately announces that she is officially "eight-and-a-half," finds the show "totally retro," a cool term she picked up from *Raven* on television. When I attempt to point out a particular gaffe in the show's dialogue, I learn that I am *super*-retro—too old to have ever been that cool.

"Just how old are you, Grandpa?" she asks, with a squinted eye.

"Fifty-nine, dear. I'm fifty-nine. Why do you want to know?"

Ashley rolls her eyes and tosses her head, a gesture that I presume is something genetic from her father's side of the family.

"That means you'd have to be a boomer like the cool guys on '70s. I want to see a birth certificate. A driver's license can be faked!" She means it, too.

"Ask your grandmother, dear, she'll tell you my age, my weight, and possibly the number of hairs I have left on my head—the same balding head she once combed and stroked and snipped a locket from while I slept."

Ashley maintains a cocked head and a skeptical look on her face.

"I'm fifty-nine. I weigh 160 pounds—same as when I got married. I still have all my own teeth *and* the same wife of thirty-five years. I was never in a rock band or in a protest march, or into drugs. I did not get a flaming red Mustang or GTO for high school graduation, and I didn't dance hip hop at my prom. I danced to the Beatles and the Stones and the Four Tops—very poorly, I admit, and I played guitar even worse. Though I could strum a few popular tunes of the time—if the moon was in the seventh house and Jupiter was aligned with Mars.

"*I could strum a few popular tunes of the time—if the moon was in the seventh house and Jupiter was aligned with Mars.*"

"No, dear, I did not hitchhike to *Frisco* for the Summer of Love, and I'm well aware I'm the only person in my generation who wasn't at Woodstock. Yes, I did join a fraternity in college, mostly jocks and *weekend* hippies. You were a social zero otherwise. And yes, I did experiment with Marlboro cigarettes and the kind of cheap wine no legitimate church would ever bless for communion. And when that didn't kill me, I figured God obviously had better plans for me. We all started out college sane as could be in our Weejuns and oxford shirts and ended up graduating in bell-bottoms and

sandals under our robes. Oh, yes, dear, the girls went from bouffant to board-straight, just like Ali McGraw in *Love Story*.

"What's that? Yes I did, but I have to tell you right up front I looked more fool than cool in disco polyester and a shag hairdo by Mr. Mario. Rock may have survived, but disco ruled—for a time at least. It's hard to believe we freely traded in our jeans and sandals for the Greg Brady line and nosebleed heels. We were a fickle bunch.

"That's about the time I met your grandmother and got married, got a house, and grew up. No, dear, Marilyn Monroe was actually *before* my time. I did have a crush on Gidget and Annette Funicello, though—before I met grandmother, of course. Yes, I suppose I could find a picture of Gidget, if you really *want* to see her.

"Now, does that about cover it? I'm fifty-nine—for three more months at least. Oh, my Lord . . . *Where have all the flowers gone?* Oh, it was nothing, dear, just an old beat-up song that popped into my head. What's that? You really want to hear the whole thing? Far out!"

I mull over the matter, wondering how I'd explain how three months to an eight-year-old and three months to a fifty-nine-year-old is a good example of what Einstein calls "relativity."

Solving Problems, Retro-Style

Karen Scalf Linamen

I used to look to new technology to solve my problems. Not anymore. I'm discovering that I can solve any problem by simply going back to the stuff I used to own. Here's an example:

Problem: My kids are spending too much time texting their friends.

Solution: Replace the keypads on their cell phones with rotary dials.

Problem: The guy at the Starbucks table next to mine is talking too loudly on his cell phone, and I'd like him to move to a table across the room.

Solution: Whip out my boom box and tell him I've got 10cc's "I'm Not in Love" on eight track and I'm not afraid to use it.

But no retro-solution has the potential to revolutionize my life more than the Rolodex I found last week in an attic box of castoffs. Trust me when I tell you that this simple little office accoutrement, this outdated data-storing widget, if you will, is going to help me reclaim my entire life.

I bought this particular Rolodex twenty years ago. It's not the little kind that holds business cards. It's the big carousel version that spins 2"x 3" cards around in some sort of rotisserie fashion, like the chicken-broasting machine at your grocer's deli. Only better, because broasted chicken never saved anyone's life. At least that I know of.

This Rolodex saved mine for a number of years.

Back in the eighties, I started using it to store all my phone numbers. Then addresses. Then birthdays and passwords and the combination to my locker at my aerobics class.

Before long, I'd added the dates of my last oil change, the names of the Cabbage Patch dolls my kids wanted for Christmas, and the recipe for homemade Play-Doh.

Soon I was going through the entire house with a laundry basket, collecting all the weird scraps of paper on which I'd written important information: the shoebox lid with directions for our Atari video game player; the table napkin with the birthdays of my niece and nephews; the used envelope on which I'd written the warranty information for my crimping iron.

I transferred the information and tossed the clutter.

Dental appointment reminder cards? Gone. The schedule for the coming opera season that I never attend but always think I will? Gone. The salvaged magazine pages I'd hung onto for two years because they contain 800-numbers for household gadgets I'm almost pretty sure I can't live without? Gone. The pamphlet

with the secret to solving the Rubik's Cube my husband bought me for our anniversary?

All gone.

In other words, I stuck *everything* in that Rolodex. Anything lying around the house was fair game. One day I spotted something on the couch that I'd missed and made a beeline for it, but my husband saw me coming and hurried outside to mow the lawn.

That simple Rolodex kept my house clutter-free for a number of years, until the day I "upgraded" to a Filofax, then a two-pound electronic organizer, and finally a smartphone.

It always seemed like a good idea at the time.

After years of learning curves, technical difficulties, and software crashes, I got frustrated. Eventually I reverted to my old ways, hanging onto random papers and writing things down on weird little scraps. Like rising floodwaters, clutter seeped, then poured back into my life.

I've been drowning ever since.

Until a few days ago. That's when I unearthed my attick box of castoffs and rediscovered the scratched and dusty Rolodex.

You know what I think? I think that newer isn't always better. That old school can still rule. And that sometimes the stuff we discarded yesterday is the very thing we still need in our lives today.

See why re-embracing this simple desktop gadget is such a big deal? It's not just a Rolodex. It's a way of life.

You just can't say that about a broasted chicken.

2-GOOD 2-BE 4-GOTTEN
Bill Gray

When I mentioned to one of my work friends that I was going to stop by my old high school to look at all the yearbooks that have pictures of me in them, she said, "Taking along an X-ACTO knife?"

I'm not one of those people who get all wrinkly nosed and red-faced when I see old pictures of myself. I know I was a weird-looking kid. I wallowed in being a weird-looking kid. Bring on the weird, I say.

So I sat for an hour today in a wooden school chair in a little room off the library, which was the gym when I was a student there, and looked at the Troy High School yearbooks from 1964 through 1970.

The first thing that struck me was how wrong people's perceptions of the 1960s are. Even mine, and I was there.

Right through to 1970, most of the boys in the yearbook

photos have short, side-parted hair, plaid shirts with button-down collars, and straight-leg jeans or slacks. Most of the girls have short perms, and although the Brenda Lee end flips were a lot more prevalent in the earlier years, they were still around in 1970. So were those pointy-cornered glasses with rhinestones on them.

Often people associate the sixties with hippies, and they associate hippies with brilliant flashes of neon color. The yearbooks are almost entirely in black and white, and it seems appropriate, like in reruns of *Leave It to Beaver* or *Father Knows Best*.

It is 1967 before a flowered shirt shows up among the madras. A year later for paisley.

I didn't grow up in a town of love-ins, peace marches, or rock festivals, but one of football games, the annual town fair, and Friday night roller-skating.

Through the 1960s, we stayed remarkably in the 1950s.

Even my friends who loved rock and roll and the Beatles almost as much as I did were a pretty conservative bunch. The primary difference between them and everyone else in the yearbook is that their hair is combed an inch down their foreheads, rather than being sharply parted to the right or left.

In the 1965 yearbook is a picture of the chess club. Three of the members were kids who played in rock and roll bands I was in. One lead guitarist was a junior high class officer. A bass player also played football.

One of the reasons I had to visit my old high school to view yearbooks was that I never bought any of them.

For me, high school was enjoyable but unimportant. Troy was just the town I was going to leave as soon as the suede cowboy boots I wore to graduation could carry me away. They didn't

understand me there. They didn't respect me there. They couldn't see what was ahead for me the way I could see it.

Let the others take over their fathers' farms, or go to Mansfield or Penn State for college, or get married and start cranking out future Troy High School graduates. I had bigger plans. My little town seemed content to pretend that there wasn't a larger world. I knew better. I wasn't reading *16 Magazine* for nothing.

I could see pictures of the cool fashions that the Ben Franklin in Troy didn't sell. I knew about Beatle cuts. I knew there were rock and roll managers out there just waiting to sign me, record companies just waiting to record me, fans just waiting to mob me.

Like so many kids in so many little towns, I resented Troy for holding me back.

So it's interesting, looking through those old yearbooks, to realize how much fun I had in school. A surprising number of my teachers were cool. I forgot that until I saw their pictures again.

It's interesting, looking through those old yearbooks, to realize how much fun I had in school.

Other photos reminded me of my completely forgotten membership in the drama club. The photos of the senior play and the senior talent show reminded me of what a great time the rehearsals were. That brought to mind my junior high production of *Romeo and Juliet,* and I grinned like a smiley button.

I thought about the poem I wrote when my English teacher asked for an essay and how she read it to the whole class. I

remembered the math teacher who taught one-to-one correspondence with such humor and enthusiasm that, to this day, I remember the phrase "one-to-one correspondence." I thought about elephant jokes and cinnamon fireballs, about doing the Twist and the Freddie in the gym, and about a pretty, blond girl in a plaid miniskirt worn over textured stockings, and held shut with a huge gold pin.

I thought of a thousand little conversations in front of lockers or in line at the chocolate-milk machines. I remembered strutting down the broken, uneven sidewalks into town while my friend Jack sang self-penned dirty versions of Top 40 songs.

After my library research, I walked down the hallways of my old school. I walked against a sea of students on the way to their next classes, and I thought about how lucky they all are.

The girls can wear pants to school instead of the skirts or dresses girls were required to wear when I attended. They can all wear shorts, which were, of course, completely unheard of in my time unless you were putting up prom decorations that day.

And they're lucky, because one of these days they'll have a fine collection of memories.

For somebody who couldn't wait to shake the dust of Troy, Pennsylvania, off my feet, I always enjoy coming back. Maybe we're not meant to know how good we have it during the actual having.

I know now.

Chapter 2

That Person in the Mirror Can't Be Me!
(Beauty and Fitness)

20 Perks of Being Over 50...

1. Kidnappers are not very interested in you.
2. No one expects you to run into a burning building.
3. People call at 9 P.M. and ask, "Did I wake you?"
4. People no longer view you as a hypochondriac.
5. There is nothing left to learn the hard way.
6. Things you buy now won't wear out.
7. In a hostage situation, you are likely to be released first.
8. You can eat dinner at 4 P.M.
9. You can do without sex, but not without your glasses.
10. You enjoy hearing about other peoples' operations.
11. You get into heated arguments about pension plans.
12. You have a party and the neighbors don't even realize it.
13. You no longer think of speed limits as a challenge.
14. You quit trying to hold your stomach in, no matter who walks by.
15. You sing along with elevator music.
16. Your eyes won't get much worse.
17. Your investment in health insurance is finally beginning to pay off.
18. Your joints are more accurate meteorologists than the National Weather Service.
19. Your secrets are safe with your friends because they can't remember them either.
20. Your supply of brain cells is finally down to manageable size.

You're as Young as You're Ever Gonna Be

Anita Renfroe

I can't believe the stuff I drop money on in the cosmetics department of Walgreens. It's that no-questions-asked return policy they have that lures me in. It makes me feel I can be a fearless shopper when it comes to makeup and toiletries. Did the shade of lipstick you chose resemble the safety cones on the roadside when you got it home? No problem. Walgreens will take it back. Did the bubble bath promise to send you into bath-time nirvana but leave you with a rash instead? No problem. Walgreens will take it back. I've had some great fearless purchases, and I've had some real doozies.

I actually bought something called "Weight Reducing Cream" in a lovely pearlescent tube. Right there on the tube is printed, "Lose Pounds and Inches" and "Controls Appetite, Increases Metabolism, Firms and Flattens." Honey, if there was somethin' in a tube that could do all that, wouldn't *you* trot it right up to

the counter and lay down your hard-earned dollars? I had visions of myself actually losing weight while sleeping or—even better—losing weight *while* eating dinner. If we live in the era of land rovers on Mars, could simultaneous eating and losing weight be too farfetched?

Well, I got the stuff home, popped the top, and just knew I was gonna be firmed and flattened by daybreak! Wasn't Oprah just gonna call me right up and ask me to be on her "Amazing Transformations" segment in a week or two? Maybe I should dig out the digital camera and take some "before" pictures just in case.

I had visions of myself actually losing weight while eating dinner.

According to the directions, I was supposed to rub a quarter-size dollop onto my tummy and "other problem areas" one hour prior to eating. (Don't they know that at a certain age, they're *all* "problem areas?") So I slathered a good palmful onto my "areas" (everything between my boobs and my knees), reasoning that if a quarter-size dollop were good, wouldn't *seven* quarters be better? I felt sure that I would shrink before I got to REM.

Problem is, I never actually got to sleep that night. I felt exactly like I had overdosed on Sudafed as I flopped like a chicken on the rotisserie all night long. I was trying to sleep but felt like a live wire still hooked up to the power plant. After three exhausting hours of this, I got up in the middle of the night with heart palpitations, certain I was having some sort of cardiac incident, and tried to read the ingredients. Only then did I notice the fine print: the actively absorbed agent was none other than caffeine.

I had smeared the equivalent of fifteen cups of coffee on my "problem areas." In this product's defense, I did lose weight from the bed gymnastics.

I believe that there's not much a girl won't do if the promise includes holding back the hands of time or erasing the marks that time has already made on her. I know I'm susceptible to the miraculous cream claims and the appeal of youth. But isn't the definition of "young" getting a good bit more youthful every year? Supermodels are told that their careers are over at the ripe old age of twenty-five.

It is hard to help my teenage daughter navigate this profoundly shallow culture. When every other television show is built around the premise of surgical enhancements and "extreme makeovers," it's a chore to convince a girl of any age that beauty is something deeper than a plastic surgeon can touch and that she radiates true beauty every time she shows love and compassion. (I wonder why we never see a TV show about that.) But I have come to a place of some acceptance in my life via the thought that no matter how old I feel, I'm as young as I'm ever gonna be. Think about that carefully: You will never be any younger than you are at this moment. Hello!

Age is relative anyway. For instance, if you are eighteen and it is your destiny to be taken from this life at the age of twenty-one, you may *think* you're young, but in reality most of your life has already been lived. That makes you old. On the other hand, if you are fifty-eight and you are going to live to be a hundred, you're young (proportionately). The point is, none of us knows how long we might live or how old that really makes us, so why not celebrate how young you might be? As Satchel Paige said, "How old would you be if you didn't know how old you are?"

43

I have known some aged people who are very young inside. Marge Caldwell from Houston is a vibrant sprite of a woman who sparkles and giggles when she talks and is going on ninety years young. She is a woman who knows that age is just a number on a driver's license. Conversely, I have known some teenagers and college students who by virtue of the weight of life upon them seemed as if they were very, very old.

This notion of today being my youngest day of the rest of my life makes me want to try to turn cartwheels, live a little more daringly, celebrate everything with a bit more gusto, and fully appreciate the gift of life. So today I will skip the caffeine body cream and maybe call a friend as I pour a second cup of fresh-brewed java.

Youth is not in a number, or in a night cream, or in a surgeon's scalpel. It's in your head and your heart. Be as mature as you must, but refuse to be any older than you are. Don't let this youngest day of the rest of your life go by without a little celebration!

Runner's High
Zarette Beard

Baby boomers are aging (big news flash, right?). Even if you hadn't already noticed, you can't miss the deluge of news items telling us so. It seems that speaking with authority on the many ways for boomers to stay fit is more important than national elections and the war in Iraq! One thing is for sure—it's big business.

When I passed forty and felt my body scurrying along the downward slope of life, all the hype started to get to me. According to the doomsayers, a lack of simple physical exercise could almost certainly shave years off my life, leave me limbless and blind from the ravages of diabetes, put enormous strain on my aging heart, leave me mentally dull and unfashionably dumpy. It was clear I needed to get with the program—any program!

After watching a news report on the benefits of long-distance running, I thought it might be just the trick. I think it was the woman who described "runner's high" who finalized my decision.

Of course, I had no intention of running across Canada like she had, but I was sure I could work up to a couple miles a day and feel like a spring chicken again.

After a few days of light jogging, I felt prepared for the big day. I took off running around the neighborhood, dressed in my professional running shoes, designer running shorts, running bra (nearly dislocated my shoulder and hyperextended my neck putting it on), specially designed sweat-wicking fabric T-shirt (complete with underarm dry shields), and matching headband. As I passed my neighbors, they all were pointing, laughing, and joyfully smiling at me. I smiled back and waved at them, touched by their support and encouragement. "Yep, smaller butt, here I come!"

Five minutes later (that's right, five minutes, go ahead and mock me), I started to cramp. Not being a quitter, I pushed through the pain like an Olympian. I had to. My neighbors were still in sight and my pride wouldn't let me stop until I got around the corner. Based on my fatigue and rapid heartbeat, I figured I was really close to achieving the aforementioned "runner's high," so I pushed myself to keep going, the theme from *Chariots of Fire* playing in my head. A little girl rode up alongside me, her pink Pretty Pony bicycle gleaming in the sun (it was the silver glitter model). I looked down at the small face with the scrunched up nose. "Lady, are you OK?" she asked, her little blond head cocked sideways. Not wanting to traumatize this child by dying on the spot, I slowed my speed to a walk. After I assured her that I was quite all right, just a little winded, she rode off, her little knees pumping up and down like twin pistons on a steam engine.

A couple more torturous trots around the neighborhood and I was ready to call it quits. "No big deal," I told myself. I'll just try something more suitable for my body type like . . .

You would not believe how happy I was when I stumbled across a book on "free weights'" at the bookstore. Yeah, man, this was the ticket.

I skimmed the workout book and immediately noticed that I was supposed to eat five meals a day! Woo hoo! I began that part right away. I was committed. The next day, I hit the weights, and they promptly hit me back. Within a few hours, my arms were too sore for me to comb my hair and I could barely walk. (Well . . . I could walk but not completely upright.) I went to work the next day looking like I had been dragged under a bus. I approached the stairs and paused at the bottom, thinking it might be time for a career change. Slowly, gingerly, I began my ascent, feeling seventy, looking ninety. A plump coworker sprinted past me on her second trip to the cafeteria that morning. My commitment to weight training ended on the spot. "Perhaps isometrics would be better," I reasoned.

Based on my fatigue and rapid heartbeat, I figured I was really close to achieving the aforementioned "runner's high".

I brought it home in a box, jubilantly ripped it open, and removed the device that was going to get my big butt into that little swimsuit. A Thigh-Buster! The model on the front looked great. An attractive, young woman was smiling and reading a book while working out. *This is my kind of exercise,* I thought. Turns out, it's trickier than it looks. I lay down on my back and assumed the gynecological position. I placed my Thigh-Buster between my knees and began to squeeze. I don't know if my thighs got a workout, but my abs, neck, and face sure did! I

could barely squeeze the thing at all. *Perhaps it's not positioned correctly,* I thought. I adjusted the thing, summoned all my strength, and squeezed again. My toy poodle, Sophie, barely escaped as my Thigh-Buster shot into the air like a missile.

Sophie was already a little nervous around workout equipment ever since the treadmill incident, which occurred during one of my earlier brushes with fitness routines. The sweet little thing jumped on while I was running on it, and that treadmill threw her backward like a rock from a slingshot. Thank goodness the big blue Exer-ball was between her and the wall. She bounced off and ran for her life, and I sold both the treadmill and Exer-ball at a garage sale a few weeks later.

Believe me, I was discouraged. I resorted to exercises I had learned in elementary school—jumping jacks, push-ups, and pretending to touch my toes. And, of course, I worked hard to maintain a good diet (five full meals a day, loaded with all the recommended daily allowances). Even with all my efforts, the numbers on my bathroom scale continued to creep upward. A close friend told me to stick with it. "You always gain a little when your fat is turning to muscle," she assured me.

Starting this week, I'm trying something new, though. I place both feet on my scale until it tries to record my weight. Then, I lift one leg to the side while leaning and stick out my arms the opposite way. I will look like a drunk figure skater with a bad sense of direction, but it just might work. I'll find out for sure when I can stay on long enough to read the number. Until then, I will continue to search for the perfect exercise.

And for the record, I still think wandering aimlessly is exercise, don't you?

Mountain Boomer

Jeff Sawyer

My pal Ferguson the plumber is my age, which is to say, born back in the day when "back in the day" was still "back in the old days." Ferg's a big, beefy guy—his Sleep Number is 259—and his good wife, Nancy, has been encouraging him to jog, work out, or do pretty much anything in the evening besides watching the *Northern Exposure* reruns he TiVos. He idolizes, and sort of resembles, the character Maurice Minnifield, a retired Mercury astronaut who became the bold entrepreneurial frontiersman of Cicely, Alaska. Ferg sees Maurice as living life unburdened by the responsibilities common to those of us in the lower forty-eight, like, say, soldering broken pipes in wet basements at two in the morning.

Ferg's talking bathroom scale recently corroborated Nancy's visual assessment of his silhouette with hard data, announcing dryly one morning, "Ten more pounds and you get your own governor." And so he did what many of us boomers do when the prospect

of declining health closes in: He delayed the inaugural breaking of sweat by launching a weeks-long investigation of every piece of fitness equipment made. Activity is not something you want to rush into.

We boomer consumers are a demographic that marketers pursue as relentlessly as ushers chasing a bat during a sermon. We're sufficiently Web-savvy to analyze their product offerings more thoroughly than any topic of any research paper we ever wrote in college, and affluent enough to more or less afford what we eventually settle on. Accidental scrutiny of my own physique one morning in my forties ("What is a *mirror* doing in a *bathroom*, honey?") led me to purchase a serious

Activity is not something you want to rush into.

rowing machine. I actually used it, three times a week for years, until a herniated disk left me frozen in the rowing position. Walk around the office with the posture of a Slinky going downstairs, and people are going to think you're feeling overburdened. Which maybe you are—and the solution to that, they'll tell you, is exercise.

Now I walk and jog on a treadmill for half an hour every other day—mostly walk, in truth. Eventually this will reduce my knees to the crunchy consistency of salad croutons, and I'll move on to the next instrument of torment, maybe something in the elliptical family, or perhaps the rack, until I'm so magnificently healthy that all of my body parts are completely worn out. But at least I'll feel good about the attempt.

On Saturday morning, Ferguson and I went down to the local big-box fitness store to scope out some equipment he'd researched online. It had a big parking lot to cross, and by the time we arrived at the doors we were frankly glad they opened themselves. The home

gyms in the place seemed to have pumped up at least as much as the people who use them. Sitting inside one, you're surrounded by pulley stations, tall stacks of chromed weight plates, ab crunchers (isn't that a Kellogg's product?), and hoists that look as if they could winch a V-8 out of an Impala. The machines come with manuals illustrated with photos of women so idyllically buff that if they were standing right there in front of you, they would not even talk to you.

The cavernous store's pallid overhead lighting made Ferg and me look even paler than we are, especially next to the artificially bronze salespeople. Surrounding us were acres of brand names that seem designed to speak to you wherever you find yourself on the exercise ladder: facing a misspelled reality (Weider), still optimistic (New Form, ProForm), sensing the urgency of the transformation ahead (Lifeline), or resigned to the inevitable (Doctor's). Whoever came up with "Orca" as the brand name of a swimsuit needs to go back and focus-group it, even if it *is* for triathlon athletes.

"You ever notice that 'exercise' and 'exorcise' are only a letter apart?" Ferguson muttered as he ambled up to a massive treadmill. I sensed ambivalence. But he bought the thing—not for the advertised horsepower, programmable routes, or shock-absorbing belt—but for the big fan in the center of the console that might alleviate the suffering that would follow. We strained to load the enormous box into the back of his pickup. "This counts as one workout," Ferg noted. Just two months later, he had set it up in his front room; and a month after that, he tried it out.

Walking the dog past Ferguson's house the other night, I spied him through the window, steaming his way up some imaginary hill on the treadmill. Bathed in the blue light of the TV, the incline set steep, he actually looked pretty determined. Almost as if he might be climbing to Alaska.

Hooked on the Ladies' Hair Journals

Marti Attoun

Every six weeks I visit the hair salon wearing the same chin-length bob that I've worn since the original George Bush and fantasize about finding a new hairstyle—something pizzazzy, but not so over-the-top that my Southern Baptist mother calls Thelma— next link on the prayer chain—on behalf of my sick hair.

I always arrive early and settle in with an open mind and a lap full of the latest glossy professional journals published by the hair industry. Truth is, I'm addicted to the hair catalogs.

It's not rational. Decades of shopping the wish books for a doable 'do for my Midwestern scalp and sensibilities should convince me that I'll still be looking like me when I walk out the door. I should just set these books down right now and catch up on *People.*

Yet, hope springs like a cowlick.

I flip the pages and—here we go again—I'm reminded that the

hair profession does not need to invest in malpractice insurance. You think your coif looks like shredded cattails after that $200 cut and perm? Before you call an attorney or the Better Business Bureau, check out page 38 in *Styles for Real People*. It's legit. It's there, right beside a style that should be captioned, "Hair run over by a John Deere while looking for a four-leaf clover."

I don't know where these "real people" live, but they sure aren't hanging out at the local Wal-Mart. I remind myself to keep a liberal attitude about layers and lengths and such and I dive back in. Surely this will be the month when I can show a photo of one of these real people to Natalie, my hairdresser, and say with the fortitude of a French knot: "Make me look like this woman, please."

Are these crowning glories or clowning glories?

I'm wide open to suggestions when I spot something familiar. There, on page nineteen, a sprigged blonde, looking flash-frozen, gazes toward Mars. It's the exact style and look I

wore after twenty-eight hours of labor and childbirth. I didn't call it "California Contemporary," though. "I called it, 'Nevermore.'"

Are these *crowning* glories or *clowning* glories?

I take a deep breath—then gasp. The most hair-raising entry yet is a dramatic "before" and "after" photo of the victim—I mean model. The "before" reminds me of Lisa, the sensible woman I dipped chili beside at the last school carnival. "Before," she wears a shoulder-length brunette flip; "after," she wears minced tangerine hair and resembles a Chia Pet with ten-day growth.

Truly, though, I sympathize with the editors of these publications, who have to compile sixty or so pages of this hair nonfiction

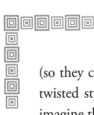

(so they claim) each month. What a challenge! Every bizarre and twisted style has already been plotted and headlined. I can only imagine the brainstorming sessions that go on:

"Let's see. In last month's book, we created gelled linguine bangs and that clever retro shag cut with pinking shears. We need a couple of page-turners like the Medusa braids and confetti sideburns in last December's book."

An associate suggests a "glitzy style, similar to garnishing the scalp with fluffy poodle tails."

The editor rolls her eyes. "Competitor has it on the cover this month."

"Then what about a scalloped awning of bangs that totally obscures both eyes and then, to draw attention sideways toward the cheekbones, two heavily sprayed poufs that resemble loofahs for the ears?"

"Been done to death," the editor says and sighs.

They bounce more outlandish ideas around the table—rooster tails, roman candles shooting up the back, vintage pincurls unfurling down the forehead and curling beside the nostrils, a Brillo-pad affair on one side only. Finally, someone suggests a kind of "gasoline rage" style for the times—shaving a two-inch band around the middle of the head to resemble a highway lane—then ratting what's left on either side into large thickets.

"Perfect!" the editor shouts. "We'll make it the cover. Now find us a hot twenty something to model it."

My wild hair imaginings are interrupted when Natalie summons me to the chair. Caught red-handed, I plop the stack of hair porn on the floor.

She snaps a plastic cape around my neck. "What are we doing this month?" she asks and picks up a hank of my hair. She stares

at it as if it holds the secrets of the universe. Maybe it does, but so far, it's not talking. "The usual trim?"

I look at my "before" in the mirror. It's the same "before" I saw six weeks before. It's the same no-frills, low-maintenance, sensible hair that has identified me for more than a decade.

I try to imagine being one of the hair-journal girls with carefree tufts or artsy tangles. Maybe I would be carefree or artsy if my hair led the way. Which comes first—the breezy bangs or the breezy behavior? The tightly coiled hair or the tightly coiled personality? The sensible hair or the sensible person?

A hair shakeup could shake up my very identity.

I could cope with the attention that one of these follicle follies would focus on no-frills, sensible me. It might even be fun, since it would be temporary. I know the hair would grow out.

Here's the scary part that keeps me addicted, window-shopping-only for now, in the hair catalogs: I don't know how fast a personality grows out.

"The usual," I tell Natalie.

Color-coded

Patsy Clairmont

"Does turning forty bother you?" Les asked on my birthday.

"You've got to be kidding. Everyone has thought I was so much older for so long, it's a relief. It makes me feel legitimate," I insisted.

"You know what I hope never happens to you?" he added wistfully.

"What?"

"I hope you never get to the point when, as you wave your hand to say good-bye, your underarm waves in the opposite direction."

"That, quite honestly, has never entered my mind," I assured him.

My husband may be prophetic, because about two weeks later, during my morning shower, every bit of tone rinsed out of my body and down the drain.

It's truly an annoying attribute to be moving in one direction and feel your body waving in response. Stopping is the challenge,

because it takes several seconds for the fleshy momentum to slow to a jiggle and finally stop. One could suffer from "whip flab" if one were not careful or stopped too quickly.

I realized that Les noticed his fear had come true when Mother's Day came that year. He bought me a set of dumbbells. Actually, mine were called "smart bells." I didn't think it was a smart move on his part. I was insulted. No, make that ticked!

Finally I decided to do the scriptural thing with my heavy gift and take the writer of Hebrews' advice, "Let us lay aside every weight . . . which doth so easily beset us. . . ." I put them in storage in my bedroom closet.

I had put other things in there never to find them again. I was hoping for that kind of fate for my "bells."

Les never mentioned that I wasn't using them. I think he knew better.

Christmas came, and the memory of my Mom's Day gift had almost faded. For a moment, though, I felt some apprehension when he handed me a beautiful package, lest I find a tummy tuck coupon book or a fanny fixer or some other anatomy adjuster.

To my delight, however, I found a multicolored dress with a shimmering fabric that was feminine and lovely. I was impressed. I was speaking at a luncheon in the area for a holiday celebration, and this would be perfect.

I still remember standing on a small platform giving the talk, "Jesus Is the Reason for the Season." To add emphasis to one of my points, I made a sweeping gesture, only to notice for the first time the dress's full draping sleeve.

That's when it hit me: Les had given me colorful camouflage. He had taken a more subtle approach to fleecing my flab. I laughed to myself and thought, *I'll get him later!*

Moose in a Noose

Sue Fagalde Lick

They were discussing thongs when I walked in. Not the rubber flip-flops we used to wear to the swimming pool, but the sexy underwear my sister-in-law calls "dental floss."

"What would you recommend for my first thong?" asked a young woman.

"Oh, I like this one," the proprietor of the lingerie shop said, holding up a frilly pink bit of lace.

"Is it really comfortable?"

"You'd be amazed. I just love mine."

"Will it cover my belly button?"

I stood in the middle of the closet-sized store, gawking at the tiny bras and panties, and felt like a moose—an aging, overweight moose.

I wanted to cut and run, but this was the only place in town to buy a smoothie, a miracle garment that would allegedly make me

look sleek and sexy under the new formal I had just bought to give a speech at a banquet. Living in a town where dressing up means putting on clean blue jeans without holes, I confess to not knowing much about formal wear. It took two hours to find a dress that didn't show too much of me and didn't make me look like the mother of the bride. Once I got it zipped up, there was my belly poking out, saying, "Look at me; I'm made out of mayonnaise." That's when the dress shop lady told me to go buy a smoothie.

There was my belly poking out, saying, "Look at me; I'm made out of mayonnaise."

The only smoothies I knew about were the milk and fruit concoctions they sell at health food stores, but I headed over to Thongville feeling hopeful.

"How can I help you?" asked the store owner, who was young enough to be my daughter.

"I need something called a smoothie to go under a formal."

"What are you trying to smooth?"

I patted my belly. "What else?"

She opened a drawer and pulled out a faded pink circle of elastic. It looked like something my grandmother wore to keep her varicose veins from popping out.

I must have blanched.

"No?" She reached back into the drawer for a shorter variation, same color, same elastic the consistency of new tires.

"Um . . ."

"Well," she said, "You could just buy the control top pantyhose that go up high."

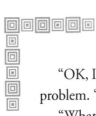

"OK, I'll try that." I was halfway out the door, but I had another problem. "I need to find a bra that won't show over my dress."

"What size do you wear?"

I looked away and mumbled "38C." She started swooshing bras past on their little hangers. Numbers flashed by: 30, 32, 34. I saw a $120 price tag. For a bra? She found my size way in the back. The garment was black, accented with scratchy gold threads. She handed me two more in similar styles and led me into the dressing room.

As I stripped off my stretchy top and my full-figure white bra, my breasts flopped downward, pointing at my rounded belly under the blue stretch pants. I picked up the first bra. It was like trying to dress a walrus. Grabbing both ends of the bra, fearful it would snap me in the face if I let go, I stretched it as far as I could. It wouldn't hook. Neither would the second. Too much me, too little bra. I got the third bra on, but it hurt, and any second it would explode, killing anyone within fifty yards.

I got dressed and opened the door. "I have to think about it," I said. I couldn't tell this thong-wearing babe that I needed something even bigger!

I went home, tried on my old bras and found one that would work under my dress if I pinned it in the right places. A trip to Wal-Mart yielded a pair of black extra-large high-rise, belly-smoothing briefs for eighteen dollars. Ugliest things you ever saw—and strong. You could carry a cord of wood in them and they wouldn't even stretch out. I added control-top pantyhose to the ensemble for double squashing action.

Yes, sir, I was going to look like a million bucks. Thank God nobody would be peeking underneath to see what was holding it all together. I guess that's why they call it Victoria's *Secret*.

PWSD (Pre-watersport Stress Disorder)

Karen Scalf Linamen

I think women are amazing; I really do.

After all, we know how to give birth, change tires, run major corporations and small kitchen appliances, raise children, mend broken hearts with chocolate, analyze our friends' marriages and even our own, cook a Thanksgiving turkey, *and* redecorate an entire house using a single charge card.

So—if I'm a woman and I've got all that going for me—how come every summer I can be induced to panic, anxiety, and insecurity by a single sentence?

Let's go to the pool.

It's not that I hate my body. The problem is that I have not been professionally airbrushed. This is the reason that, whenever I put on a swimsuit, I don't look like the models in the magazines who *have* been professionally airbrushed. Diet, genes, and personal trainers have nothing to do with it. I have no doubt that,

61

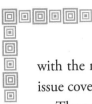
with the right airbrush artist, the next *Sports Illustrated* swimsuit issue cover girl could be Rosanne Barr.

The other reason I dread the words "Let's go to the pool" has to do with the little-known problem of anxiety disorders common to Spandex. Every springtime, as I pull last year's swimsuit out of the drawer where it spent the winter, I can see immediately that it has developed a very hostile attitude, most likely due to separation anxiety.

Separation anxiety has been studied in children and even pets, but behavioral scientists have yet to turn their attention to the symptoms of this common anxiety disorder as exhibited by seasonal clothing. In this state of mind, a swimsuit will turn on us and do any-thing—including shrinking two sizes over the winter—to make our bodies appear as unattractive as possible.

Under this kind of pressure, is it any surprise we turn to chocolate?

When this happens, if you can't find a textile therapist willing to help your swimsuit work through its issues, you may have no choice but to see your relationship for what it was—a summer fling—and put yourself back in the marketplace for a new suit.

The process of seeking a relationship with a new swimsuit can be intimidating. You may experience rejection. You may feel self-conscious and awkward at times. You may spot a promising candidate across a crowded rack, only to be disappointed when, upon closer inspection, it becomes obvious that the two of you are not a good fit.

The whole experience can be extremely stressful.

This is why women don't shop for swimsuits in groups. It's just not a fun girl group event. We do *other* things in groups. We go to tea rooms together. We go garage sale-ing together. When we're at restaurants, we even visit the powder room together. But I can't tell you the last time I went bathing suit shopping with a friend. We also don't get root canals together, and we don't schedule a 'girls' night out to get unwanted facial hairs zapped via electrolysis together. So you can see, really, the kind of unpleasant category the whole swimsuit-shopping thing falls into.

No wonder we get stressed just *thinking* about those five little summertime words, "Let's go to the pool."

Under this kind of pressure, is it any surprise we turn to chocolate?

Well, not just chocolate. As an equal-opportunity emotional eater, when I'm stressed or anxious I also turn to Twinkies, pretzels, and ice cream straight from the carton.

Although not at the pool. At the pool I try to avoid any food that melts, which is why I usually eat fruit. I love strawberries, but slices of watermelon are my all-time favorite. And a glass of iced peach tea or a cold can of Fresca is always welcome. Grapes are another refreshing poolside snack. Besides, the fruit theme goes well with coconut-scented sunscreen, don't you think? And doesn't that scent always evoke the greatest memories? Of course, when we were unsuspecting kids we used oil—no sunscreen allowed—but the smell was the same. I can't even *think* about that coconut scent without feeling the warm sun on my skin, hearing laughter and splashing, reliving the delicious shock of easing myself into the cool water in the heat of the day.

And melting. Remember that melting thing your muscles start

63

to do when you're basking at the edge of the water? Or after an afternoon of splashing and swimming?

Come to think of it, I never stress-eat on afternoons like those. Maybe it's because—when I'm finally there, enjoying all that sunshine and water—I'm never stressed.

This might be a good thing to keep in mind as I get ready for summer. After all, if I spent more time thinking about *why* I go to the pool (instead of whether I have what it takes to pursue a career in the swimsuit model industry) maybe I could relax a little. Have a little more fun. Smile more. Enjoy all that sun and fun. Be healthier in body and in attitude, too.

Besides, by not becoming a highly paid swimsuit model, I may actually *save* money. I hear those extreme makeovers by airbrush don't come cheap.

Exercising Our Prerogative?

Martha Bolton

They say our metabolism slows down during middle age. Mine didn't just slow down. It pulled over and parked. No matter what I do, I can't seem to get it to shift into gear and take to the road again. It's perfectly content to sit there on the shoulder of life's highway and watch the world go by. Meanwhile, every morsel I eat attaches itself to my frame and hangs on like a barnacle on the *Queen Mary*.

The answer? Some say it's exercise. Regular exercise is supposed to increase the body's metabolism and help it burn off all those extra calories that we happen to take in throughout our day.

But I for one have never been very fond of exercise. I have enough night sweats. Why would I want to sweat during the day too?

Exercising with equipment holds the least appeal for me. Sure, the TV ads make the rowing machines and various other types of equipment look easy. You don't see anyone huffing and puffing

and begging for oxygen. The spokespeople simply do their work-out, pat their cheeks and foreheads with a hand towel, and tell you how much it will cost (plus shipping and handling) to have one of their miracle machines in the privacy of your home.

Now, I might find working out on exercise equipment a little more tempting if there were a better incentive than merely losing weight. If I'm going to work that hard on a machine, I want something worthwhile at the other end of all my stretching. In other words, I'd gladly do the Gazelle or the AB Slide if there were a box of yummy donuts just slightly out of my reach. I'd have no problem at all walking on a treadmill if there were a hot fudge sundae staring back at me from the opposite end of the conveyor belt. Real incentives—that's what I need. Merely visualizing myself in a pair of size eight jeans isn't enough anymore. I need tangible rewards, rewards I can see, feel, and cover with whipped cream and nuts.

Exercise videos and television programs don't motivate me either. I don't like all the yelling.

"Get off that sofa and get moving!" the trainer barks.

First of all, I'm not usually sitting on the sofa. I'm laid out on the recliner. There is a difference. Second of all, why can't she ask nicely? When you're already so out of shape that one sit-up takes half the afternoon, who wants a drill sergeant making you feel bad about it? The way I see it, if someone wants me to twist and bend my body into contortions that have never before been seen or imagined, there had better be a "pretty please" attached.

I don't know about you, but I don't need any more guilt. I already feel guilty enough every time I take my fork up to the dessert bar at the buffet and skip the plate. (Oh, like nobody else has ever thought of doing that?)

And anyway, it's not like I don't get any exercise at all. I walk to my mailbox every day, and on some days I have had to look all over the family room for the remote, and who knows how many steps I take doing that? I do knee bends getting the Fritos that I keep on the bottom shelf of the cupboard and shoulder stretches reaching up for the Breyers in the top freezer. I'd like to see someone come out with a video featuring these kinds of exercises.

I need tangible rewards, rewards I can see, feel, and cover with whipped cream and nuts.

But I'm not completely convinced we should be burning all these calories, anyway. How do we know it's a good thing? Has anyone ever researched where all these burned calories are going and what they might be doing to our environment? What if burned

calories are, in fact, what's messing up the ozone layer? What if it isn't hair spray at all? What if one day we discover that calories are something we were supposed to keep with us, not go sending off willy nilly into the atmosphere?

Until more research is done on exactly where all these spent calories are going and how the loss of them is affecting our world, I choose to limit my incineration of the little guys. It's not that I'm lazy. I'm patriotic. Wait, no, it's more than patriotism. This is a much higher calling. This has global significance. This could be yet another world-changing idea. I shall clear space in my office for my second Pulitzer. And I shall set an example to all others by vowing to burn only a handful of calories every day. It's the very least I can do to save the world.

Chapter

For Better or for Worse
(Marriage)

"What Is This?"

An Amish boy and his father, visiting a mall, were amazed by almost everything they saw, but especially by two shiny silver walls that could move apart and then slide back together again.

The boy asked, "What is this, Father?"

The father (never having seen an elevator) responded, "Son, I have never seen anything like this in my life. I don't know what it is."

While the boy and his father were watching with amazement, a heavy old lady in a wheelchair rolled up to the moving walls and pressed a button. The walls opened and the lady rolled between them into a small room. The walls closed and the boy and his father watched the small circular numbers above the walls light up sequentially.

They continued to watch until it reached the last number and then the numbers began to light in the reverse order. Finally the walls opened up again and a gorgeous, voluptuous twenty-four-year-old blond woman stepped out.

The father, not taking his eyes off the young woman, said quietly to his son, "Go get your mother."

"Do You Know This Man—
'Cause I Certainly Don't!"

Gwendolyn Mitchell Diaz

On a recent Friday morning, a distinguished gentleman was spotted entering a local café with a group of businessmen. They were deeply engrossed in a discussion concerning several upcoming performances of the Imperial Symphony. The gentleman in question was overheard asking where advanced tickets for the opera *The Elixir of Love* could be purchased.

As they entered the restaurant, it was noticed that he was carrying a jar of salsa in one hand and a cup of Pero in the other. He ordered an Egg Beater omelet and lavishly ladled the salsa on top. He explained that he hasn't eaten meat in close to six years and loves the tangy taste of salsa. He also avoids caffeine at all costs—hence the Pero.

When he emerged from the restaurant an hour or so later, the subject under surveillance adeptly attached a Bluetooth receiver to one ear while inserting an iPod Shuffle in the other. A laptop

was slung over one shoulder, and he was typing a message into his Blackberry.

Several of our friends passing nearby somehow mistook this gentleman for my husband. As a matter of fact, they informed me that they have often seen Ed entering or exiting Claire's Café on Friday mornings in the same manner.

I adamantly contend that they are wrong. As much as this man may look like my husband, he is an imposter!

The man I married more than thirty-five years ago was definitely not a culinary connoisseur. He loved eating greasy bacon with his very real eggs, and coffee surged through his veins. Ketchup was his condiment of choice.

And the one time I broached the possibility of purchasing tickets to an opera, my then newlywed husband replied, "No way, unless it's being performed at half-time during an NFL football game!"

The techno-geek often seen emerging from Claire's Café is obviously a charlatan. The man whose papers I typed in college once swore that he would go to his grave never having turned on a computer. And not long ago he insisted that his fingers were far too big to ever dial a cell phone.

Besides, the man I married had raven black hair and a dark mustache. The man in question was described as a silver fox.

Mixed Messages
Patsy Clairmont

When our big twenty-fifth anniversary arrived, Les bought me nothing. Of course that's what I had asked for, but what does that have to do with anything? Mates are supposed to be able to decipher mixed messages. Les is supposed to distinguish when I mean "absolutely no" from when I mean "sort of no."

Here's the thing. Wives don't want to shoulder the responsibility of giving husbands permission to be extravagant. It frees us from guilt if we say no and our husbands don't listen to us, which of course is what we're hoping will happen. That way we can say to others, "I told him not to do this, but he did it anyway."

Les and I agreed to take a trip south as a shared gift, but I was hoping for something a little more personal. I must have been too convincing when I said, "If you get me anything I'll be mad." Maybe I should have said, "If you get me anything I might, in a minute way, be temporarily displeased."

73

Most of us gals secretly hope for a good "show and tell" kind of gift, especially for our twenty-fifth. It's difficult to flaunt—I mean to show—a trip to your friends.

I decided to subtly retract my giftless declaration at the first appropriate moment.

A week later Les dropped me off for a speaking engagement and announced he was going to the area mall for his morning coffee. The word "mall" flashed like a neon opportunity.

With more zeal and clarity than I meant to display, I blurted out, "Why don't you buy me something!"

Oops, I probably confused him by being that . . . that . . . honest. Not that I'm not always honest . . . sort of.

When Les came back to pick me up, he had heard the message, for there, on the front seat, was a beautifully wrapped gift. I admired it for a moment and then began to remove the floral paper. Inside were layers of soft white tissue secured with a gold seal that read "lingerie."

Well, this was proof that honesty did pay; I was getting what I deserved. So what if it was a week late.

I gently pulled back the last layer of tissue and lifted out my . . . my . . . prehistoric gift. What unfolded was a long white cotton nightshirt sporting a gregarious dinosaur, which wore a lopsided hat.

This truth thing, girls—you'll need to be more specific!

Taking Tea Down Under
Elece Hollis

Some husbands aren't good at choosing gifts—this is a revelation, right? Gifting was one of *The Five Love Languages* Gary Chapman lists in his book by that name. I found Chapman's book bursting with truth and verification, in writing, that Ron ought to buy me more presents. Chapman says people express love in different ways. Ron's language may have been affirmation, but mine, I'd decided, was getting stuff.

Don't get me wrong. Ron is a loving husband who has been generous with flowers and chocolates and has even given me wonderful gifts such as a fine set of iron skillets for Christmas, so who can complain?

The glitch truthfully was based in jealousy. My husband's job required travel—most of it in winter, while my job—mothering seven children, required only travel to places like the grocery store and dental offices.

So when Ron began planning for a second trip to Australia, the Land Down Under, I was a teensy bit jealous. I whipped out my copy of *The Five Love Languages*, which had caused nearly as much discord in our marriage as preparing our wills

There is really nothing a woman likes less than money she can't spend.

and trying to decide who would be blessed with our children to raise should we both expire at the same time. With the book in hand, I pointed out to Ron (very sweetly, of course) that he should bring me a gift from Aussie Land.

Usually, when he arrived home from an out-of-the-country trip, he would bring us foreign coins and bills. While I found the money interesting, if he'd thought about it much, he'd have realized that there is really nothing a woman likes less than money she can't spend.

"Things should change," I declared, and this trip would be a good time to begin. Ron claimed that the trouble was that, although he traveled to many cool places, he worked there and wasn't out sightseeing, where he would encounter places to buy souvenirs and gifts.

Ron was excited about this trip and would be carrying along conference materials, so would only have one suitcase for clothing. A friend told him to roll his underwear tightly like burritos and fit those socks and T-shirts into plastic Ziploc bags to conserve space in his suitcase.

The two weeks passed slowly. We didn't hear from Ron much. I was lonesome and bemoaning the fact that *nothing* fun ever

happened to me—right up to the day when Ron was scheduled to return home.

After supper he rolled his suitcase into the middle of the living room, and announced jovially that he had brought gifts for everyone.

"We'll see," I inwardly grumbled from my spot on the couch. The children gathered around while Dad produced coloring books with Australian animals, bright picture books, a tin of Koala brand tea leaves, a jar of Vegemite with a bright yellow lid, a tiny silver kangaroo, some nasty black licorice in a small white paper bag, and boomerangs for the boys to break windows with.

The tea and the candy were for me, but I was not impressed. Then he pulled from his suitcase a Ziploc bag with underwear rolled up inside. "Here is your present, Elece," he said with a grin of satisfaction.

"Oh, yeah—you travel around the world, and I get your dirty laundry—No thanks," I said, and as he moved away I tossed the bag to him, "I don't want your old present."

Ron jumped and grabbed the package looking as dismayed as if I had spurned the crown jewels.

"You don't understand that this is your present," he repeated stepping closer and laying the underwear in my lap.

"I understand perfectly, and I don't want your old undies!" I countered.

He turned back from mid-room and said, "But it is a gift from Australia, from Down Under."

I tossed the package at him, "No, it is not! It's your idea of a joke, and you can keep it!"

Ron lunged and caught the flying parcel in midair and stared

blankly at me. He blinked and then sighed. Carrying the package back and laying it carefully in my lap, he repeated, "This is your gift. I wrapped it for you so it wouldn't get broken in my luggage. I went to great trouble to get it for you. Please take it."

I waited until he had crossed the room and then casually tossed it toward the center of the floor. Ron dived for it like a quarterback after a fumbled football in the end zone, and scooped it up just before it hit the carpet.

With a sigh, he unzipped the bag and pulled out a T-shirt and unrolled it to reveal an object in bubble wrap. Removing the bubble wrap and some tissue paper, he unwrapped a lovely hand-painted china teapot—a real beauty—miraculously unharmed.

I gasped and then knew what he had been trying to show me all along. The underwear had protected the teapot. It had not broken, chipped, or cracked, although I felt like a genuine crackpot.

I polished the teapot and set it out of harm's way inside my china cabinet. It is a prized possession. I show it off to all my friends and relatives, affectionately referring to it as my Down Underwear teapot. Koala tea, anyone? It is delightful with roast crow.

Lois...What's Her Name?

Marnie Macauley

It recently occurred to me that life is a lot like geometry. We're just one Euclidian mess of circles or worse, parallel lines facing south and never meeting. (Hey, math wasn't my strong suit. Or gym.)

A few weeks ago I asked my brother in Arizona if my one-and-a-half-year-old nephew was talking yet, and he said no. "But he *points.*"

That night my husband and I were watching a *Seinfeld* rerun, and we proceeded to have the following conversation:

Him: "Look! Isn't that . . . you know . . . the one on *Superman?*"

Me: "Lois Lane? What's she doing on a *Seinfeld* rerun?"

Him: "I don't think she's 'Lois' here. So . . . what's her name?"

Me: "Noel Neill . . . She played opposite George Reeves . . . 1954 to 57."

Him: "Not the movie . . . on TV."

Me: "Oh, right! I just saw a whole show with her on it."

Him: "So . . . what's her name?"

Me: ". . . beats me."

In desperation, we called the twentysomething son from his cave. We both point. He gives us the "glue factory" look, mumbles "Teri Hatcher—*Desperate Housewives,*" then disappears, shaking his head, no doubt computing the relative cost of putting us in "the home," with or without indoor plumbing.

Whoever said we lose a trillion brain cells a second, should add we lose them *all* the day we turn forty. Face it. When you're donning an umbrella and acting out "Singing in the Rain" because you can't remember the word "salt," you either have a tumor . . . or you're getting older.

No doubt about it, my brain is leaking more fluid than a two-month-old infant on Enfamil—or a ninety-year-old geezer on Ensure. (For which we may purchase both Pampers and Depends. Is my circle theory getting to you?)

Of course the uplifting news is that I can remember things that happened in 1959 without a problem. Ask me the name of my kindergarten teacher, all the words to "Venus," the entire cast list of *Where the Boys Are,* and on which show Arnold Stang clucked, "What a chunk a chocolate!" during a commercial break (*Mr. Peepers*), and I'll reel them off like a jabberwocky from Where-Are-They-Now-Who-Cares-Anyway-Boomer-Mensa. But ask me to recall what I had for breakfast, and I'll play charades like a rabid mime or stare in a stupor until you lead me off—pointing.

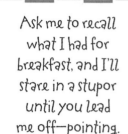

Take, for example, Liam Neeson and Ralph Fiennes. Now I know they must be different. Both were in *Schindler's List* and sometimes even in the same scenes. But you could hold me hostage (without my Wrinkle-B-Gone or yak placenta), and I couldn't pick out Liam from Ralph. I do know that one of them is married to Ralph Richardson's daughter—or is it Tony—and one played Charles Van Doren, but which?

Ask me to recall what I had for breakfast, and I'll stare in a stupor until you lead me off—pointing.

As for the bad boys, I can't tell a Sheen from a Sheen or a Baldwin from a Baldwin or a Sheen from a Baldwin and would throw them all in jail whenever one tosses a minibar (or a size two Q-tip with hair) out of a hotel window.

As for the good girls. Fortunately, we've solved the problem. We "simplify!"

Me: "Oh, look, *Sleepless in Seattle* is on tonight. Isn't that the one with—"
Him: "No. That's the other one."
Me: "The one married to one of the—"
Him: "Right. So . . . ?"
Me: "The blond one."
Him: "Thanks, hon."

We've simply reduced all the Megs, Sharons, Michelles, Kims, and Heathers to "the blond one."

You see, this is no mere boomer-harangue. Many Gen Xers

often wonder what could possibly keep two tired boomers together for more than twenty-five years after they've witnessed, said, smelled, and heard things that would drive any sane person to a cavern in Sri Lanka.

This is why. I believe there's a method to this biologically induced amnesia. The reason has nothing to do with shared memories of labor rooms, diaper pails, ERs, spit-up, SATs, death wishes—or even loyalty. No.

The singular reason we don't split is because who else are we going to get to finish our sentences for us? Do you have any idea how much work it would be to break in someone new?

Why the only person I'd be able to commune with would be my nephew, the Pointer.

Chapter 4

The Perilous View from the Top
(Perspective on Life)

Does It Work?

A druggist was promoting the new super-improved Rogaine hair restorer when a customer asked if it was really effective. "I'll say!" replied the pharmacist. "Yesterday a lady wanted some for her husband. She opened the safety cap with her teeth and this morning, she called to say she had a mustache."

View from the Web

Robert Fulghum

This is my neighbor. Nice lady. Coming out of her front door, on her way to work and in her "looking good" mode. She's locking the door now and picking up her daily luggage: purse, lunch bag, gym bag for aerobics, and the garbage bucket to take out. She turns, sees me, gives me the big, smiling hello, takes three steps across her front porch. And goes, "AAAAAAAAGGGGGGGGH HHHHHHH!!!!" (*That's a direct quote.*) At about the level of a fire engine at full cry. Spider web! She has walked full force into a spider web. And the pressing question, of course: Just where is the spider *now*?

She flings her baggage in all directions. And at the same time does a high-kick, jitterbug sort of dance—like a mating stork in crazed heat. Clutches at her face and hair and goes, "AAAAAAAAGGGGG GGGHHHHHHHHH!!!!" at a new level of intensity. Tries opening the front door without unlocking it. Tries again. Breaks key in the

lock. Runs around the house, headed for the back door. Doppler effect of "AAAAAAAAGGGGGGGGGHHHHHHHH . . ."

Now a different view of this scene. Here is the spider. Rather ordinary, medium gray, middle-age lady spider. She's been up since before dawn working on her web, and all is well. Nice day, no wind, dew point just right to keep things sticky. She's out checking the moorings and thinking about the

It's the web thing that I envy. Imagine what it would be like if people were equipped like spiders.

little gnats she'd like to have for breakfast. Feeling good. Ready for action. All of a sudden—earthquake, tornado, volcano. The web is torn loose and a huge piece of raw, but painted, meat is making a sound the spider has never heard before: "AAAAAAAAG GGGGGGGGHHHHHHHHH!!!!" It's too big to wrap up and eat later, and it's moving too much to hold down. Jump for it? Hang on and hope? Dig in?

Human being. She has caught a human being. And the pressing question is, of course: Where is it going and what will it do when it gets there?

The neighbor lady thinks the spider is about the size of a lobster and has big rubber lips and poisonous fangs. The neighbor lady will probably strip to the skin and take a full shower and shampoo just to make sure it's gone—and then put on a whole new outfit to make certain she is not inhabited.

The spider? Well, if she survives all this, she will really have something to talk about—the one that got away was THIS BIG. "And you should have seen the JAWS on the thing!"

Spiders. Amazing creatures. Been around maybe 350 mil-

lion years, so they can cope with about anything. Lots of them, too—sixty or seventy thousand per suburban acre. It's the web thing that I envy. Imagine what it would be like if people were equipped like spiders. If we had this little six-nozzled aperture right at the base of our spine and we could make yards of something like glass fiber with it. Wrapping packages would be a cinch! Mountain climbing would never be the same. Think of the Olympic events. And mating and child rearing would take on new dimensions. Well, you take it from there. It boggles the mind. Cleaning up human-sized webs would be a mess, on the other hand.

All this reminds me of a song I know. And you know, too. And your parents and your children, they know. About the eensy-weensy spider. Went up the waterspout. Down came the rain and washed the spider out. Out came the sun and dried up all the rain. And the eensy-weensy spider went up the spout again. You probably know the motions, too.

What's the deal here? Why do we all know that song? Why do we keep passing it on to our kids? Especially when it puts spiders in such a favorable light? Nobody goes "AAAAAAAAGGGGGG GGHHHHHHHH!!!" when they sing it. Maybe because it puts the life adventure in such clear and simple terms. The small creature is alive and looks for adventure. Here's the drainpipe—a long tunnel going up toward some light. The spider doesn't even think about it—it just goes. Disaster befalls it—rain, flood, powerful forces. And the spider is knocked down and out beyond where it started. Does the spider say, "Forget that?" No. Sun comes out—clears things up—dries off the spider. And the small creature goes over to the drainpipe and looks up and thinks it *really* wants to know what is up there. It's a little wiser now—checks the

sky first, looks for better toeholds, says a spider prayer, and heads up through mystery toward the light and wherever.

Living things have been doing just that for a long, long time—through every kind of disaster and setback and catastrophe. We are survivors. And we teach our kids about that. And maybe spiders tell their kids about it, too, in their spider sort of way.

So the neighbor lady will survive and be a little wiser coming out the door on her way to work. And the spider, if it lives, will do likewise. And if not, well, there are lots more spiders, and the word gets around. Especially when the word is "AAAAAAAAGGGGGGGGGHHHHHHHH!!!"

Looking for Love on the Wrong Planet

Cherie Rayburn

I've never before believed in aliens. I mean, I saw that TV special on the Roswell autopsies, and call me a skeptic, but I swear it looked just like the kind of thing you see at any Halloween fun house, only in grainy black and white.

Several months ago, I heard from a friend of a friend that a guy I used to date got married (we'll call him "Fred"). Not that I ever seriously considered marrying Fred myself—he was way too attached to his mother (we'll call her "Dot"). I tried my darndest to make a relationship with Fred work, but I just couldn't get past a recurring nightmare: me in the hospital, my third day of hard labor bringing our eleven-pound baby into the world. The phone rings. It's Dot with a true emergency—she can't get the lid off a jar of pickles. Fred kisses me on my sweaty forehead and says, "Keep up the good work. See ya later?"

Like I said, not that I ever thought marriage to Fred would

work for me, but I certainly didn't want him to marry someone else. (It's a girl thing.) And I particularly did not want him to marry someone like *her* (we'll call her "The Other Woman"). She's a beautiful, perky blonde, years younger than me. And I'm not making this up—she's a surgeon. (Oh great, brains and money too!) The ultimate humiliation is, she's popular, a member of *this* humanitarian board and *that* philanthropic committee, recipient of award after award for selfless acts of compassion, and a regular in the local society pages.

The week I learned Fred had finally extinguished his torch for me, to marry The Other Woman, I found myself in that place single, fortysomething women often find themselves—watching videos with my cat and downing a quart of Chunky Monkey ice cream. I fought the urge through *Sleepless in Seattle* and half of *Casablanca* before I gave in and did something I never, ever in a million years thought I would do. I joined the ranks of the pathetically desperate—yes, I logged onto an online matchmaking service.

But, I told myself, this is not just any matchmaking service (we'll call it "e-happilyeverafter.com"). I've seen their commercials. They show starry-eyed, hopelessly in love couples, along with the notice, "These are not actors. They were once losers like you, doomed to a miserable, lonely life until we saved them through our ultra-scientific matching system."

Who can argue with a scientifically matched date? Here's the way e-happilyeverafter.com works: You take the free, no-obligation personality assessment. They run the results through their database of opposite-sex assessments. They match you on a gazillion points of compatibility, and e-mail you the happy results of your online search for the perfect man. The catch: If

you actually want to communicate with Prince Charming, you have to pay.

Fortunately, there's a plan to fit every budget, and all credit cards are accepted. It's brilliant marketing, actually. They tell you you've been matched with "blank" number of men, any one of whom could be an ideal soul mate and father of your children, then spring the membership fee on you. "Yes, Joe Perfect has been waiting all his life to meet you—will that be Visa or MasterCard?"

I figured, what the heck? I was fed up with well-meaning, happily married friends who said, "It was when I gave up looking for a man that God brought what's-his-name into my life." Really, if I had a nickel for every time I've heard that, I could buy my very own young, attractive surgeon. I was more than ready for e-happilyeverafter.com and the scientific method! Besides, it didn't cost anything to take the personality assessment (a $50 value!).

After an hour and a half of intense self-analysis and ice cream consumption, I was worn out.

It was a good thing I had all of Friday evening ahead of me, with no anticipated interruptions, like annoying phone calls from male admirers.

The e-happilyeverafter personality assessment was a real time commitment, longer than most of the relationships I've had. (Maybe that's my problem.) Nevertheless, I attacked it with zeal, taking survey after survey, finding out stuff about myself that I never knew before. Believe it or not, before e-happilyeverafter, I had never once in my whole life analyzed whether I like board games (1) only a little, (2) somewhat, (3) moderately, (4) a lot, or (5) with a passion. Talk about scientific!

After an hour and a half of intense self-analysis and ice cream consumption, I was worn out. But I was in the home stretch. I could almost feel Joe Perfect blowing in my ear. Only a couple more questions to go, including "How far are you willing to search for your once-in-a-lifetime love? Accompanying this question were choices such as "within my zip code only," "within my metropolitan area," "within my state." I checked the option "anywhere in the whole entire world." And to make sure the scientific method rooted out every man "in the whole entire world" compatible with *moi*, I also checked "I will accept all ethnicities as matches." No sir, I didn't want to miss any Antonio Banderases out there.

I paced the floor after nervously pressing "enter," sending my personality assessment into the amazing e-happilyeverafter matching machine. In return, I received the message "Congratulations! In just a few minutes, you will receive an extensive list of handsome, successful, single men each guaranteed to make Fred insanely jealous."

Sure enough, only a couple of minutes later, it arrived—the message upon which nothing less than my future happiness depended. It said, "We're so sorry, but it appears that there is absolutely no one in our database that you're compatible with." I was stunned. All I could think was, "Oh, my gosh, my mother was right!" I swallowed hard and read on: "Don't worry, we get new people all the time, and odds are really good that we'll find that perfect someone for you before you're 90. But you want to be ready when Mr. Right finally rolls up in his wheelchair, so join today—will that be Visa or MasterCard?"

So much for science. Three months later, I'm still not compatible with anyone in the whole entire world. I did, however,

recently receive a notice from the e-happilyeverafter folks that read, "Sorry, we still haven't found anyone who can put up with you. Perhaps you should consider broadening your geographical parameters for the search."

Bingo! All this time, I thought Mr. Perfect had to be an earth-ling! Nope, according to the love experts at e-happilyeverafter. com, my search can be expanded to beings not of this world. I immediately wrote back "YES! Feel free to expand the search for my soul mate to whatever planet in whatever galaxy your service covers." Needless to say, I am relieved to know that there's really nothing wrong with me. I've just been looking for love on the wrong planet. (I wonder if Martians like Chunky Monkey and board games?)

Things We Still Don't Know
After All These Years

Martha Bolton

If we're living life right, we're supposed to get smarter over time. We make mistakes and learn our lessons. We try one thing, and if it doesn't work, we try something else. We pick the wrong friends and learn to pick better ones next time. We grow. We mature. For most women, time is our teacher.

But time doesn't answer all our questions. Some things we still don't know after all these years—things that baffled us in our youth or young adult years and are still baffling us today. Times may change, but these mysteries haven't, and I don't know about you, but as a woman I would really like to know the answer to the following:

- Just what was it Billie Joe McAlister threw off the Tallahatchie Bridge?

- Are the single socks we lose in the washing machine the same single socks I find by the curb while jogging? (This is obviously a trick question. Me? Jog?)

- Why did it take Susan Lucci so long to win a Daytime Emmy?

- Why are we called the weaker sex when some of us have been known to give birth to six babies in the same day?

- What in the world was Seinfeld thinking with that final episode?

- What does compounded interest really mean, and why does it amount to only four cents on my savings account statement?

- What is the correct translation of "Do wah diddy diddy dum diddy do?"

- Who really shot JR? I'm still not buying the dream thing.

- What is Cool Whip made of, and why does it never melt?

- Just how tan can George Hamilton get before being officially considered deep-fried?

No Batteries

Robert Fulghum

Could I share a rule with you? It is not my rule, necessarily. It came from a very grumpy-looking man at a holiday office party. A man coming down with a full-blown case of Scrooge-itis. He had just unwrapped his dinky little present from under the office tree. In tones of amused sorrow, he said to nobody in particular:

"You know, it's not true that what counts is the thought and not the gift. It just isn't true. My mother was pulling my leg on that one. I have collected so much gift-wrapped trash over the years from people who copped out and hurriedly bought a little plastic cheapie to give under the protective flag of good *thoughts*. I tell you, it is the *gift* that counts. On rather, people who think good *thoughts* give good *gifts*. It ought to be a rule—the *Brass Rule of Gift Exchange*."

And he stomped off toward a garbage can carrying his little gift as if it were a dead roach.

Well, maybe so. It's a kind of harsh judgment, and a little close for comfort. But the spirit of the season has been clear for a long time. God, who, it is said, started all this, cared enough to send the very best. On more than one occasion. And the Wise Men did not come bearing tacky knickknacks. Even old Santa, when he's making his list, is checking it twice. And the angels came bringing Good News, which was not about a half-price sale.

I do know what I want someone to give me for Christmas; I've known since I was forty years old.

I do know what I want someone to give me for Christmas; I've known since I was forty years old. Wind-up mechanical toys that make noises and go round and round and do funny

things. No batteries. Toys that need me to help them out from time to time. The old-fashioned tin ones I had as a child. That's what I want. Nobody believes me. That's what I want, I tell you.

Well, okay, that's close, but not quite exactly it. It's delight and simplicity that I want. Foolishness and fantasy and noise. Angels and miracles and wonder and innocence and magic. That's closer to what I want.

It's harder to talk about, but what I *really, really, really* want for Christmas is just this:

I want to be five years old again for an hour.

I want to laugh a lot and cry a lot.

I want to be picked up and rocked to sleep in someone's arms, and carried up to bed just one more time.

I know what I really want for Christmas.

I want my childhood back.

Nobody is going to give me that. I might give at least the memory of it to myself if I try. I know it doesn't make sense, but since when is Christmas about sense, anyway? It is about a child of long ago and far away, and it is about the child now—in you and me. Waiting behind the door of our hearts for something wonderful to happen. A child who is impractical, unrealistic, simpleminded, and terribly vulnerable to joy. A child who does not need or want or understand gifts of socks or potholders.

The Brass Rule is true.

Chapter 5

Who Are These People?
(Children)

A Letter to Bubba

Dear Bubba,

I have been unable to sleep since I broke off your engagement to my daughter. Will you forgive and forget?

I was much too sensitive about your Mohawk, tattoo, and pierced nose. I now realize that motorcycles aren't really that dangerous, and I really should not have reacted that way to the fact that you have never held a job. I am sure, too, that some other very nice people live under the bridge in the park.

Sure, my daughter is only eighteen and wants to marry you instead of going to Harvard on full scholarship. After all, you can't learn everything about life from books.

I sometimes forget how backward I can be. I was wrong. I was a fool. I have now come to my senses, and you have my full blessing to marry my daughter.

Sincerely,
Your future father-in-law

P.S.: Congratulations on winning this week's lottery.

Be It Ever So Rent Free

Bill Cosby

More and more children these days are moving back home a decade or two after they have stopped being children because the schools have been making the mistake of teaching Robert Frost, who said, "Home is the place where, when you go there, they have to take you in." Why don't they teach *You Can't Go Home Again* instead?

I recently met a man and woman who had been married for fifty years, and they told me a story with enough horror for Brian DePalma. Their forty-six-year-old son had just moved back in with them, bringing his two kids, one who was twenty-three and one who was twenty-two. All three of them were out of work.

"And that," I told my wife, "is why there is death."

Who wants to be seven hundred years old and look out the window and see your six-hundred-year-old son coming home to live with you? Bringing his two four-hundred-year-old kids.

I have five children, and I love them as much as a father possibly could, but I confess that I have an extra bit of appreciation for my nine-year-old.

"Why do you love her so much?" the other kids keep asking me.

And I reply, "Because she's the last one. And I never thought that would occur. If I'm still alive when she leaves at eighteen, my golden age can finally begin."

I find there is almost music to whatever this child does, for, whatever she does, it's the last time I will have to be a witness to that event. She could set the house on fire and I would say, "Well, that's the last time the house will burn down."

"If I'm still alive when she leaves at eighteen, my golden age can finally begin."

She is as bad as the others, this nine-year-old; in fact, she learns faster how to be bad; but I still look at her with that extra bit of appreciation, and I also smile a lot because she is the final one.

I sympathize with the older ones for not understanding. They are perplexed because things they did that annoyed me are now adorable when done by the nine-year-old. When the older ones took pages from the script I was writing and used them for origami, I was annoyed; but when the last one does it, I feel good all over.

After their last one has grown up, many fathers think that the golden age of solitude has arrived, but it turns out to be fool's gold, for their married children have this habit of getting divorced, and then they drop off the children at your house while they go to find another spouse.

And sometimes it is not only the children, but animals too.

"Dad, I wonder if you could watch our horse while we're away."

"Well, what if your mother and I decide to go someplace?" you say.

"You people are old. You don't go anywhere."

The only reason we had children was to give them love and wisdom and then freedom. But it's a package deal: the first two have to lead to the third. Freedom—the thing so precious to Thomas Jefferson. He didn't want his kids coming back either, especially because he had six of them.

In spite of all the scientific knowledge to date, I have to say that the human animal cannot be the most intelligent one on earth because he is the only one who allows his offspring to come back home. Look at anything that gives birth: Eventually it will run and hide. After a while, even a mother elephant will run away from its child and hide. And when you consider how hard it is for a mother elephant to hide, you can appreciate the depth of her motivation.

Buy the Book

Carol McAdoo Rehme

Throughout our parenting years, my husband and I read everything we could get our hands on—popular baby magazines, church literature, pediatrician pamphlets, Dr. Spock—determined to parent by the book.

And we took the expert advice we read. We sterilized; we purchased safety-tested, doctor-recommended car seats; we locked away dangerous cleaning solvents. We studied each new stage as our child grew: the terrible twos, puberty, adolescence. Until we reached a new stage: teenager.

And our teen had discovered cars.

"Don't worry," my husband comforted. "I read an article, 'Parenting Teenagers,' and it said to let your child *earn* the money for his first vehicle. It will be years and years before Kyle can afford anything."

Meanwhile, Kyle was doing his own reading: *Blue Book* and the classifieds. And my husband was wrong. It didn't take years and years to afford something, because Kyle found a "bargain." A used Jeep. His dream car.

The vehicle was a bargain because previously it was owned by another teenage boy who obviously never read anything. He drove the Jeep without oil. Check in hand, Kyle raced out to make his purchase and promptly . . . towed it home.

How could I ever trust the safety of my once securely seat-belted child to such a flimsy vehicle?

Have you ever really looked at a twenty-eight-year-old Jeep?

Up close?

It was put together with zippers and snaps. I'd seen Matchbox cars that looked sturdier. Had I known exactly what Kyle wanted, I would have offered to *stitch* him a vehicle. How could I ever

trust the safety of my once securely seat-belted child to such a flimsy vehicle? It was a decade older than he was, and it didn't even run!

And, Kyle, who had never ever changed a spark plug, was going to install an entire engine?

"Don't worry," my husband reassured. "The owner's manual came with the Jeep. We'll let him study it out and tinker with this awhile. He'll never be able to take it to college. It will be ages and ages before his Jeep is roadworthy."

With bad weather settling in, the Jeep was shoved into the garage—my stall, of course—where it took up residency. For the entire winter.

Meanwhile, Kyle rolled up his shirtsleeves and began dismantling it. If it was loose, he wiggled it off. If it had pieces, he separated them. If it could be removed, he disassembled it. We were reminded of his Lego years. Only now the pieces were bigger. Costlier. Greasier.

Soon, the Jeep bled onto the other side of the garage (his dad's stall this time). My husband was right. It had been ages and ages, and still the Jeep wasn't running.

"Don't worry," Kyle soothed. "I'll just hoist in this rebuilt engine, and you'll have your garage back in no time."

Then he consulted experts of his own. Strange boys in dirty sneakers and sweaty T-shirts huddled over the Jeep. Parts catalogs, engine diagrams, and wiring manuals littered the kitchen counter. Margarine tubs housed Jeep . . . entrails. And there were peculiar odors and loud noises and greasy fingerprints. Everywhere.

Meanwhile, I consulted a how-to book of my own, *Keeping a Clean Nest*, and memorized the chapter on stain removal. Did you know that teenage boys leave grease on everything? Refrigerator doors, milk jugs, showers, sinks, light switch plates, ceilings, and . . . toilet seats.

This job was bigger than Baby Wipes. I unlocked every cleaning solvent we owned. I tried everything. Some things worked better than others.

It was a long winter.

But, wonder of wonders, one fine spring day the slumbering Jeep stretched and yawned, grumbled a little, then rolled from its winter bed. We held our breaths when—after several false starts—Kyle coaxed it from hibernation.

We heaved a joyous sigh of relief. At last, the end of a stage.

The Jeep was out and going, the house grease-free, the garage once again our own.

Now Kyle would leave the safety of our home for college. Driving a . . . decrepit vehicle . . . with a carburetor that hiccupped . . . and an engine that stuttered. When it was running at all.

So, run we did—to the nearest bookstore. After all, now we needed to buy a new how-to manual for a new stage, *Surviving an Empty Nest.*

Mother-of-the-Bride Blues

Elece Hollis

When my daughter Rachel announced she was planning her wedding for August, I knew immediately that I was in big trouble. Where in the world could I find a mother-of-the-bride maternity dress? One glance at the garments displayed in the woman-with-child department of the nearest clothing store was all I needed to convince me of the futility of my search. They just don't make 'em, you know?

Still, I had to find something suitable. I was forty-three and would turn forty-four before the baby arrived in November. I'd be six months along by the wedding day—no way could I hide the embarrassing, yet wonderful, fact that the beautiful dark-haired bride was expecting a new baby sister.

Pregnancies are supposed to happen to younger women. By our ages, my husband and I were supposed to know better. But we were boomers after all. Our parents were the ones obsessed

with conventionality. We played by our own rules. So I went shopping for maternity wear designed for "mature" women.

I started at a formal and tux shop. The saleslady showed me a swanky black dress with a fitted bodice tied with a leopard-print sash. No—just not me. She showed me a pale yellow satin gown with sequins ornamenting the cuffs and neckline. I tried it on. The full skirt swirled around my legs. Looking back at me from the mirror was a startled moose with jaundice.

How about a fire-engine red, knee-length gown with huge white zigzags running this way and that? Nah—I'd look like a distraught candy cane on steroids. I also passed up a pea green dress with a fitted camouflage-print jacket, rhinestones, and matching clutch purse.

Pink chiffon with loads of ruffled lace and a huge satin bow that hung down over the belly? Ugh! No way! Talk about a fashion victim.

Plans for the wedding proceeded nicely. Invitations were mailed. A three-tiered cake was ordered from a local bakery for the reception. Rachel was so excited—so happy.

We had a rice bag party and tied red velveteen ribbons on two hundred rice bags. We ordered flowers for the church, boutonnieres for ushers, candle lighters, and groomsmen; and corsages for the pianist and servers. And one for Mama—Big Mama, who still had no dress to pin it to.

I checked out my closet to see what might do if worse came to worse. Way in the back was a deep rose-colored maternity dress with a white collar I had bought to wear during my last pregnancy—a mother-of-the-graduate maternity dress. (Yeah, you read that right.) It was only three years old. Maybe it could be resurrected. But, when I laid it out, I saw the large round oily stain on the backside.

One tired mom, six months along, at the graduation celebration, I had plopped my caboose down in the nearest chair and felt the splat as I landed on a plate of cake with yummy white frosting with dark-blue lettering.

"Oh, no, Mama," squealed my ten-year-old son, "You sat on my cake!"

"I realize that," I answered (rather calmly considering), "and I am not getting up until all these people leave!" The stain had never come out. Why had I saved the dress anyway? Good grief!

On a trip to the mall to find some of that white frou-frou sheer net material to swag the tables in the reception hall, I noticed across from the fabric store, a small maternity shop named Motherhood. Motherhood—that was me—double dosing it! I went across to look around inside. You never know, and things were getting desperate.

Don't all moms feel awkward and strange at their daughter's weddings, like they'd stepped out of a time machine into another world?

There I found it at last—a robin-egg-blue, ankle-length maternity dress, with short sleeves and a scooped, lace-trimmed bodice. It was not one of the wedding theme colors, but wouldn't clash. It wasn't fancy, but it fit. It would do. I bought it.

I felt conspicuous being escorted down the aisle that August to my seat of honor at the front of the sanctuary. I'm certain some of the guests were duly horrified, but what did I care? Don't all moms feel awkward and strange at their daughter's weddings, like they'd stepped out

of a time machine into another world? Don't they all feel self-conscious and fat and a little old? Well, this day certainly wasn't about me anyway.

As I watched my girl come in on her daddy's arm, and listened as she and her groom exchanged their marriage vows, I think I felt little Sis's firm kick of approval. I smoothed my mother-of-the-bride blue skirt and patted my blessing.

Recharging an Old Battery
Randy Richardson

"Ladies and gentlemen," the ring announcer droned, "in this corner, weighing in at a slightly pudgy-but-still-respectable-for-his-age one hundred and fifty-five pounds, Big Daddy."

"And in the other corner, weighing in at thirty-four pounds, the featherweight champion of the Family Boxing Federation, The Kid."

You already know who wins this boxing match, right?

The Kid, of course. The undefeated, undisputed, undersized FBF titleholder.

It would be an upset of stunning proportions if Big Daddy were to win one of these fights, real or imagined, akin to the Washington Generals defeating the Harlem Globetrotters.

I thought about that as I nursed a bloody nose one night when The Kid's four-year-old fist met Big Daddy's schnoz, an admittedly large and sensitive target. The blow was accidental,

coming during a nightly wrestling ritual with The Kid, but it stung nonetheless.

We always hear about all the bumps and bruises that little ones endure. What we often forget is that parents take a lot of hits, too. Our hair gets pulled and we pull out our own hair, leaving many of us with much less on top than before we had kids.

You don't realize just how grown up you really are until you have a kid. I'd imagine that is even more so today than it was when I was a kid. You hear of more and more couples having children at later stages in their lives. I'm one of those. I was twice the age my father was when he became a father.

We like to say things like "I'm a kid wrapped in an adult body" or "I feel like a kid again." But aren't we really just, ahem, kidding ourselves?

As much as we like to think of ourselves as kids, our bodies and our hearts are always there to remind us that we're grown up.

I suppose I knew this all along, but the realization hit me the hardest while engaged in a little friendly jousting.

You don't realize just how grown up you really are until you have a kid.

Jousting, the competition between two knights on horseback, wherein one knight tries to knock the other off his mount, was at one time the sport equivalent to soccer in Europe or football in the United States. But that was about eight hundred years ago.

Try to explain that to a toddler, though, and all you'll get is an empty stare, followed by, "Come on, Daddy, joust."

So between my legs goes a makeshift horse, which is, in reality,

a cardboard tube left over from wrapping paper. In my right hand goes a makeshift lance, which, in reality, is also a cardboard tube left over from wrapping paper. I am, almost always, Bad Knight.

About thirty feet away is the condensed version of me, about three feet shorter but packing about ten times the energy. He is, almost always, Good Knight.

Our eyes meet. We raise our lances. And then, in unison, we call out, "Charge!"

Almost always, the battle ends with Daddy in the moat, which also happens to be the cat's water bowl. The cat is not a fan of jousting.

There are things you do as a parent that before you became a parent you would have sworn you'd never do. Jousting is one of those things.

I liked thinking of myself as a kid at heart. But the lesson I've learned from jousting is that I am an adult in both body and spirit. Not only do my knees creak when I struggle to get up after being knocked down, but I also lack the heart of an honorable knight.

While I stand there holding a cardboard tube between my legs, I find myself frequently turning my head, just checking to see if any of the neighbors can see me through the sliding glass door.

Lately I look for excuses not to joust. "Not right now," I tell the Good Knight, "Daddy's washing dishes." Yes, I'd rather wash dishes.

The Good Knight looks down, dejected for a brief moment, but then returns those battle-worn eyes to mine with that childlike glimmer of hope and throws the dagger-like response: "After?"

Beaten once again, I sigh and surrender to his magical powers over me.

After the last dish is washed, I stride to the horse stable, which is, in reality, a large wicker basket. I pull out my trusty steed and grab hold of my lance. The Good Knight beams as we square off on opposite sides of the room. Finally, we raise our makeshift lances and call out that one word the Good Knight has been waiting to hear all day: "Charge!"

By the time my boy reaches age eighteen, I'll be pushing sixty. I just hope that there's enough juice left in this old battery to take all the charges that will be coming my way over the next fourteen years.

Hail to Thee, Bankruptcy
Bill Cosby

I have always put the highest value on education. However, one day last year, my eighteen-year-old daughter came in and told my wife and me that she had decided not to go to college because she was in love with a boy named Alan.

At first, my wife and I went crazy.

"What?" I cried. "You're standing there and telling your mother and me that you're *not* going to—"

And then a light went on in one of the musty corners of my mind: Her decision would be saving me a hundred thousand dollars.

"—not going to college, which you have every *right* to tell us. Alan, you say? Well, he just happens to be the one I'm exceptionally fond of. I hope he's feeling well. Would you like me to send him to Palm Beach for a couple of weeks to get a little sun?"

A father like me with five children faces the terrifying prospect of sending five to college. When my oldest one went, the bill for

her first year had already reached thirteen thousand dollars. I looked hard at this bill and then said to her, "Thirteen thousand dollars. Will you be the only student?"

I am lucky enough to make a lot of money; but to the average American father today, thirteen thousand dollars (which has now gone up to seventeen) is more than just a sum of money: It is the need for a winning lottery ticket.

When I saw my oldest daughter's first college bill, I multiplied thirteen thousand times four, added another thirty thousand for incidentals during these four years, and got the sum of eighty-two thousand dollars that I would be spending to see my daughter pick up a liberal arts degree, which would qualify her to come back home.

The college said that if my wife and I really cared for our child, we would pay another three hundred for the gourmet special.

You think I'm exaggerating that extra expense for incidentals? For her freshman year, I had to spend another seventeen hundred for a tiny room just a quarter mile from a toilet. And then the college said that if my wife and I really cared for our child, we would pay another three hundred for the gourmet special. We wound up sending another five hundred to our daughter personally so that she would not have to eat the gourmet special but could get pizza instead.

"Dad, the food is terrible," she kept saying.

"But I enrolled you in *gourmet* food," I said.

"That's worse than the other. I want pizza."

And then, on top of the five hundred dollars a year that we

sent for pizza, we also had to keep flying her home because her clothes kept getting dirty. She was studious, so she was unable to remember to wash her clothes. She simply flew them home every few weeks and put ten thousand dollars' worth of laundry into our washing machine.

At this college, my daughter did not major in mathematics. *No* children learn mathematics at college, even when they take the courses; I have never met a college student who knows how to count. You give one of them a certain amount of money and a budget precisely broken down to cover all her expenses.

"This is for this," you say, "and this is for that."

The child listens carefully and calls you forty-eight hours later to say she is broke.

"And, Dad, the telephone company is being really *unreasonable*."

"Did you pay the bill?"

"We're certainly *planning* to. And *still* they want to turn it off."

"But I *gave* you enough—there's money in your *budget* for the telephone bill."

"Oh, we used that money for important things."

In my daughter's sophomore year, one of these important things was housing: she and her roommates decided that they just had to have their own apartment. They no longer could stand living in the dorm, where the shortsighted dean had objected to their putting up pictures of naked people playing guitars.

The eighty thousand dollars you will be spending for college might not leave you quite so depressed if you knew that the school's curriculum were solid. I am afraid, however, that the curriculum has turned to cottage cheese.

When I went to college, I sometimes cut classes to go to

the movies; but today the movies are the *class*—sorry, The Film Experience. There are also such challenging courses as the History of Western Belching, the Philosophy of Making Applesauce, and Advanced Lawn Mover Maintenance. It is no surprise to hear a college student say on his graduation day, "Hopefully, I will be able to make an input. College was a fun time, but hopefully now I'll have a viable interface with software." The software is his *brain.* The degree he is truly qualified to be given is one in Liberal Semiliteracy.

I do not mean to sound stuffy or old-fashioned. I just feel that for eighty thousand dollars, a student should spend four years in a school where English comes up from time to time. I cannot stand to see it being scaled down to the students. The students should be reaching up to it because success in life demands the use of intellect under pressure. Also knowing how to spell.

A freshman today will change his schedule if he finds he has signed up for a course that requires books. He wants courses that will enable him to both sleep late and get rich, so he will test his intellect with such things as the Origins of the Sandbox, American National Holidays, and the Principles and Practices of Billing.

I may have mentioned my feeling about grade school teachers who keep saying, "He can do the work." My feeling is that if only one of these teachers would call the boy a certified idiot, I would say, "Fine; we'll get someone to work with him." Well, in college the teachers don't say, "He can do the work." They say, "What kind of work would he like to do?" And it is this new trend of letting students shape their own curriculum that leads a student to tell his advisor, "I'd like to study the number of times every day that the average light at the intersection turns green. I want to major in Traffic."

119

Chapter 6

Who's Watching Mom and Dad?
(Aging Parents)

Divorcing After 45 Years

An elderly man in Phoenix calls his son in New York and says, "I hate to ruin your day, but I have to tell you that your mother and I are divorcing; forty-five years of misery is enough."

"Pop, what are you talking about?" the son screams.

"We can't stand the sight of each other any longer," the old man says. "We're sick of each other, and I'm sick of talking about this, so you call your sister in Chicago and tell her," and he hangs up.

Frantic, the son calls his sister, who explodes on the phone, "No way they're getting divorced," she shouts, "I'll take care of this."

She calls Phoenix immediately, and screams at the old man, "You are *not* getting divorced! Don't do a single thing until I get there. I'm calling my brother back, and we'll both be there tomorrow. Until then, don't do a thing, *do you hear me?*" and hangs up.

The old man hangs up his phone and turns to his wife. "OK," he says, "They're coming for Christmas and paying their own airfares."

Living in Life's Twilight Zone
Elece Hollis

For days now I have been Linda. My mother-in-law is so forgetful—old age? She calls me by the wrong name. But then I am prone to the same trick. I call my children by their brother's and sister's names. I just start at the top and work my way down. Sometimes, I begin with my own siblings: Kent, Fred, Jo, Ann—you know your name!

Last night mom tries to tell me something, "You know the one?" she asks.

"Not really."

"You know the one over there?" She points vaguely toward the back room, the garden, downtown, or Mecca.

"I'm not sure who you mean," I answer.

"Well, you know—the one with hair!"

"Oh, Betty," I guess vaguely, thinking of the woman I know with the poofy hair who works at the dentist's office. Now there is a woman with hair!

"No, no, no—the one I'm thinking of. You know!" I start randomly suggesting the names of her friends. "The one who makes all the noise. You know!" She insists. I start listing off my kids and grandchildren.

"Stop guessing. You only make me forget worse." Turns out she was trying to tell me something about my daughter's pet donkey. Close? Well, no. Poor thing.

At least my memory is intact most of the time.

Like that day last month (or was it last year?) when I actually remembered a good two-thirds of the items on my shopping list that I had carefully written and left at home on the kitchen countertop.

I stared out at the car—my car, and wondered where I was.

Mom and I drove to the shoe store in Tulsa one day, and she thought we were in Kentucky; we had driven so long and so far. "What state *are* we in then?" She demanded in a strained voice.

"The state of confusion, I think, but don't worry, we'll get home in time for supper."

Now, here I was in confusion again—but this time it was my own. Rushing out of the hardware store, I climbed into the driver's seat of my car and digging my key ring out of my purse, I stuck a key into the ignition. At least, I tried to, but the key refused to go in. I checked to see if I was using the house key or the trunk key. No, it was the ignition key. Well, goodness, what was the deal? Maybe I was losing it.

I sat back against the seat with a sigh of frustration. I had never had this particular car trouble before. I was baffled. I knew it was the right key. I had driven the car to this store, right? It was the only car key I had.

Then I saw my car—the one I thought I was in—parked right next to the one I was in. What could be happening? *Twilight Zone* music started playing on the radio—the radio that wasn't on. Do-do-do-do-Do-do-do-do-Do-do-do-do . . .

I stared out at the car—my car, and wondered where I was. I remembered an article I had read about near-death experiences where a guy saw his body on an operating table while he floated near the ceiling. Spoooooky.

The car I was in was mine, but it wasn't mine. Looking around inside and feeling a bit dazed, I saw this vehicle was exactly like mine—with just a few different amenities. I had a cute kitty cat pillow for Gram on the passenger seat, and my Bible had been left there since I was heading to church later—no Bible. This car held change in the cup holder instead of my favorite blue coffee cup and a box of tissues in the right seat.

Shaking myself from my stunned state, I quickly climbed out of the car. Headlines flashed through my mind's eye "Bible-toting Granny Arrested for Attempted Car Theft." "Middle-aged Lady with Cognitive Disorder Found Wandering in Parking Lot."

Good thing for me the duplicate car was as old as mine—no car alarm had blurted out my folly—same model, same color, same everything. How odd! Of all the cars, someone in a blue Oldsmobile station wagon had pulled in and parked right beside me.

I wondered if the driver had noticed the match. Looking up at the store front, I noted a man wrestling an awkward package through the door with his back toward me. He turned just as I backed out and flashing an alarm yelled out, "Hey!"

"Hum . . ." I said to myself as I drove away, another resident of the state of confusion.

Say What?
Polly D. Boyette

My mom is hard of hearing, and that can make conversations difficult, especially on the phone. A while back, my sister, Robbie, and I went away for the weekend to a resort in Manteo, North Carolina, called Pirate's Cove. I decided to give my mother a call to let her know where we were and give her the telephone number in case she needed to get in touch with us. Our conversation went something like this:

"Hello, Mom, it's Polly. Are you doing OK today?" I ask.

"Yes, I'm fine," she answers.

"Robbie and I are going on a little vacation trip," I tell her.

"You and Robbie—trip?" she answers. "Where are you going? Is it a business trip? Did someone die?"

"No, Mom, nothing like that." I'm already feeling a little frustrated. "We just want to get away for the weekend and have some fun."

"Fun?" Mom says like the concept is new to her.

I decide to move on.

"Mom, do you have something to write with?" I say calmly. "I want to give you the information about where we're staying."

"Yes," she answers quickly.

A full minute of rustling around.

"Mom?" I finally say.

"OK, I'm ready," she assures me.

"OK. The name of the place where we're staying is called Pirate's Cove."

"What?"

"Pirate's Cove," I bring my voice up a notch and repeat it.

"Cigarette Grove?" she shouts back at me.

"*No*, Mom. Honestly! Pirate's Cove not Cigarette Grove."

"What?"

"Mom, I'm going to spell it for you. Are you ready?"

"OK, I'm ready to write it down—make sure to speak slowly."

I took a deep breath and proceeded to spell out Pirate's Cove for her.

"Mom, the first word is pirate. It's P as in Paul. I as in Irvin, R as in Robert, A as in Andy, T as in Tom, E as in Edward. The second word is Cove. It's C, as in Charlie, O as in Oscar, V as in Victor, and E as in Edward. Pirate's Cove. Do you have that?" I ask.

"Yes, I think I have it. But Polly, who are all these men you're staying with?" she says with a strong tone of disapproval in her voice.

"What? What men are you talking about, Mom?"

"You know, the ones you just told me about, Paul, Robert,

127

Tom, and Edward, and all them others. What kind of weekend are you and Robbie planning? I didn't raise you like that," she scolds.

"Oh, Mom, for heaven's sake. You've got it all wrong. I was just spelling the name of the place to you. It's Pirate's Cove. P as in Paul, I as in Irvin—"

"I don't care where you're staying," Mom interrupts. "You've got no business down there with all those men. You come home right now. A fine example you're setting for your sister."

Robbie is having a great time with this—holding her stomach, laughing so hard, she's crying. I give her my best "out of patience" look and offer her the phone, but she ignores me.

"Seriously, Mom! Just write down the number." I give it to her three times before she gets it right.

I think Mom still believes we had a wild party that weekend. I'll never convince her otherwise.

> "You've got no business down there with all those men."

I sometimes don't hear so well myself, these days. I once managed to carry on a whole conversation with someone without realizing we were talking about two completely different subjects.

What he said: "I have two parrots."

What I heard: "I have two parents." (I thought: big deal, two parents. He seemed amazed that I also had two parrots.)

What he said: "I had a male and a female. What were yours?"

What I said: "The same, of course." (I'm thinking this guy is a little strange.)

What he said: "However, one of my parrots recently died."

What I heard: "One of my parents recently died."

What I said: "One of my parents recently died, too."

What he said: "That's amazing. What was the cause of death?"

What I said: "He had a cerebral hemorrhage." (I had lost my dad a couple of years earlier.)

What he said: "Your parrot had a cerebral hemorrhage?"

What I said: "Yes."

What he said: "Wow, that's pretty bizarre."

What I said: "Well, not really. I don't believe it's that uncommon or strange." (I'm feeling a little insulted now.) "How did yours die?"

What he said: He just stopped eating and dropped dead." (Hum . . . I'm thinking that sounds more bizarre than a cerebral hemorrhage.)

You see, communication is a strange thing. That's communication, C as in Charlie—oh, never mind. I don't want to go there again. Mom may be listening.

I'm Alive!

Charlene Ann Baumbich

When I check in to drive for the senior-citizens' hot-meal program, I pick up a map, individual cards concerning special instructions for clients, and, of course, the food.

The directives may vary. "Don't knock, go right in." "Enter on the west side and leave the food on the counter." "Hard of hearing." "Two sacks instead of one." Sometimes, in the more condensed apartments, I might be told, "If she's not home, knock on 235."

One day I received a new route. I sat in my car studying the cards so I wouldn't miss important cues, and one card stood out. It had a huge asterisk and the message, "He is ninety-eight." That's all I needed to dream up various scenarios, the most obvious being that I would be the lucky one to try to deliver meatloaf and mashed potatoes to someone who expired in the night.

When I pulled into the circle drive in front of his home, I

was given a peek into his personality. There were lawn ornaments everywhere. Animals, signs, posters, shiny things. It was like a little wonderland, and I smiled. I opened the container, grabbed the oven mitt, selected one of the foil-covered dishes, and sat it on the car roof. Then I opened the cooler and picked out the paper bag with his name on it. My hands were full by the time I got to the door, but I found a way to knock.

And then I waited.

And then I knocked a little harder.

And then I waited.

And then my heart started racing. I tried to discern my new course of action. Look in the windows? Get to a pay phone (before my cellphone dies) and call 911? Start screaming for help? Call the hot meals facility?

Just before hyperventilating, I heard a rustling noise and the door opened—ever so slowly. At last a small man appeared with a twinkle in his eyes.

"I'm alive!" he bellowed, as loudly as his frailty can manage.

"And no one is happier about that than me," I assured him.

He collected the food from my hands and thanked me. I found myself wishing this was the last stop on my route because I would have liked to have stopped to chat for a while with this man who still knew how to make the heart sing. This lively, aged person who had a wonderful sense of humor. This gentle soul who understood that everyone delivering food to his home must worry about the same thing.

"I'm alive!" May I never forget to celebrate that fact and pass on that beatific angel's message.

Chapter 7

Embracing Bingo!
(Aging and Health)

A Tip for Remembering

"I know I'm getting older," someone told me recently, "because I keep making mental notes to myself and then forgetting where I put them!" Another person solved the mental-note problem by writing things down. "Now I write down everything I want to remember," he said. "That way, instead of spending a lot of time trying to remember what I wrote down, I spend the time looking for the paper where I wrote it!"

Al Sanders

It's My Birthday
Bill Gray

Like many days a person anticipates in life, my fiftieth birthday was kind of an anti-climatic.

Certainly, there were high points.

The day started with a big, shiny "You're fifty!" balloon and a birthday cake—one of which we ate for breakfast.

And, of course, my wife and I went someplace special and romantic for dinner, assuming you consider being in the middle of the woods, surrounded by Cub Scouts, special and romantic.

My birthday fell during Scout Day-Camp Week, and the actual day was parents' night at the camp. Like our pioneer ancestors, we bought subs and chips and forged a trail to the campsite. I ate my turkey with fat-free honey mustard while sitting on the sub wrapper, tilting backward downhill in the dirt, listening to

sweaty, mud-encrusted, laughing seven-year-old boys telling us about their day at camp.

If I have to tell you that I loved it, then you haven't been paying attention.

After our repast, we followed the boys down a narrow, jagged trail through the woods, even though all the moms were wearing sandals. At the end of the path, we stood on a ledge that looked out over a river, and got nervous when the boys got too close to a wire strung a good five feet from the edge. On the way back, my wife found a tick on her sleeve. There were signs along the trail identifying leaves, and I leaned in close to read one: "Poison Ivy."

There were signs along the trail identifying leaves, and I leaned in close to read one: "Poison Ivy."

Back home, while Aaron showered off the topsoil he'd brought home on his person, I took the dog out for his nightly sniff 'n' spray.

I often talk to myself while walking the dog, and this night I tried out different inflections to use when I told people I was fifty.

There was the "I know! I can't believe it either!" tone of voice. Then I tried the "Oh, I'm fifty, but it doesn't really mean anything" inflection. There was the "Bummer, man" resigned-to-the-awful-truth tone. There was the self-mocking "just call me geezer" laugh.

None of them sounded quite correct. Fortunately, I walk the dog every night and will have lots of time to get it right before I turn fifty-one.

After that, it was quarter to ten, and since a fiftieth birthday

only comes once in a lifetime, I decided to spend the rest of mine doing something I would really enjoy.

I went to sleep for the night . . .

After several months of writing and reflecting about turning fifty, I think I'm finally ready to answer the question, "What does all this mean?"

And here's the answer.

I dunno.

But I've found myself thinking about two words from my favorite novel quite a bit over the past several days.

"Thou mayest."

In John Steinbeck's *East of Eden,* two characters have a debate over two words in the Old Testament. The debate centers over whether a Hebrew word should be translated "Thou shalt" or "Thou mayest."

I've been spending a lot of time lately worrying about "can" and "can't" and "able" and "unable." Will I still be able at fifty to do all the things I could do at thirty?

Maybe that's the wrong question.

A better question might be, "Do I still want to do all the things I could do at thirty, even if I can?"

Or am I old enough now to know that life isn't a contest that you have to win, but a celebration you can choose to enjoy?

If the first two-thirds of my life were spent trying to do all that I could, maybe the last third might be better spent choosing to do things that I know are important and right.

Too much of my past, I suspect, was spent worrying about things that didn't really matter and chasing things I didn't really need, while the important things were right in front of my eyes the whole time.

Family. Friends. Love.

Health. Home. Faith.

Life.

I think part of my inability to answer the big "What's it all about?" question is that I'm just not ready yet. I don't know enough. Perhaps I never will.

So in that unique way that boomers have of avoiding the difficult, I'm leaning toward replacing that one with a different question, too.

What's next?

We made love, not war; gave peace a chance; tuned in, turned on, and dropped out; and shook our groove thang.

Now what? I don't know the answer to that question, either. But I'm excited about finding it.

Please Excuse My Purchase. I Was Insane

Marti Attoun

I edged up to the sales clerk while clutching my bag with the fringed lavender sweater in it. She smiled, looked me in the eye as outlined in the customer service manual, then asked that guilt-trigger question: "Reason for return?"

This is always a moral tug of war for me because I pride myself in being an honest person. I can willfully lie and mumble, "Wrong size," which fits every store's merchandise return policy, or I can tell the truth—which as we know, can be complicated, involving the psyche, the guests on Oprah, the carburetor that just blew, and everything else. These honest-to-goodness reasons for return are way beyond the boundaries of acceptability. Not without calling a store manager, anyway, or maybe even the corporate office.

I longed to share the truth with this sympathetic-looking clerk. I needed to tell her that buyer's remorse overwhelmed me

the minute my sassy daughter smirked and said I looked like a dancing lampshade in the sweater. But nowhere on the return form that she handed me did I see a place to check, "Resembles animated shabby-chic decor." And, by golly, I didn't want store credit. I wanted a full refund.

I'm ready for a women's store that can handle the truth.

I'm ready for a women's store that can handle the truth. Sure, they all preach customer service, but show me one that hires a full-time customer confessor to listen to our tales of temporary shopper's insanity. This could do more for women's mental health and well-being than all the St. John's Wort in Asia.

If that's impractical, then at least the store should revise the merchandise return policy to include these perfectly valid reasons for return.

Check appropriate box:

_____ I thought it'd make me look like Catherine Zeta-Jones. Not a chance.

_____ On second thought, I decided I could use the money more wisely, such as on groceries.

_____ I had just listened to a John Denver song on the oldies station, which put me in an outdoorsy "Rocky Mountain High" mood. Now I realize that I don't need Gore-tex hiking boots for my city's sidewalks.

_____ I was in a hurry because the store was closing in three minutes and I felt an urgency to buy *something*.

_____ I bought it to reward myself for sticking to my low-fat diet. Today, I visited Sonic and ordered a paper boatful of extra-cheesy, greasy tater tots. I can't in good faith keep this reward.

_____ It went out of style fifteen minutes after I bought it.

_____ When I bought this straw hat on a whim, I was feeling frivolous and carefree. Now I feel downtrodden and over-wrought, and the last thing I want to do is prance around like Rebecca of Sunnybrook Farm.

_____ Would you believe that I saw a clone of this being mod-eled on "Fashion Victim of the Week" in *National Enquirer*?

_____ It was damp and dreary outside when I bought this tropical print sundress to lift my spirits. Today, the sun is blaz-ing, and besides, I realized that I'd need to remove several ribs before I could zip the dress up.

_____ It's not me. Not at this moment, anyway.

_____ The clerk insisted that these Spandex shorts were flat-tering. My best friend, who doesn't survive on commission, looked at my caboose and said it resembled two cats trying to fight their way out of a paper bag.

_____ It was half off. I was the other half off.

_____ Something must be wrong with the store lighting in the dressing room because this blouse wasn't the color of bruised mushroom when I bought it.

_____ I was feeling uncharacteristically sophisticated when I bought this cashmere suit. Today, I feel like Ma Kettle.

_____ The day I bought this leopard-print jumpsuit, my horoscope said to be receptive to offbeat and outlandish suggestions. Today, it says to be wary of foolish investments.

_____ Buyer simply blew it. Can I please try again?

The return form needs to include a blank page or two for additional and more detailed journaling about temporary shopper's insanity, for those of us who long to unburden ourselves and be 100 percent forthright.

At the bottom of the form, the honest consumer should be able to sign her name and be rewarded with sympathy, forgiveness—and a full refund, of course.

The goal of the large print books - is to allow aging baby boomers to read without the assistance

Large-print Books
Brad Dickson

Thanks to advances in publishing, guys will soon be able to read large-print books while sitting in our recliners on the weekend. A group of major publishers recently announced a line of large-print-edition paperbacks for people over forty. This is an extremely wise business decision, as the market should be tremendous. Estimates say that by the year 2020, 33 percent of Americans will be age sixty-five or older.

The goal of the large-print books is to allow aging baby boomers to read without the assistance of reading glasses. Which is a good idea. Most middle-age men would rather be seen in support hose than in reading glasses.

Reading glasses are an obvious sign of aging. My former employer, Jay Leno, regularly wears reading glasses in the office that make him look like a cross between Ebenezer Scrooge and a lantern-jawed Grandma Moses. In all the years of doing the

program, he never appeared on camera in his reading glasses for fear that viewers would mistake the show for *The Tonight Show with Grandma Moses*, which might scare off the coveted youth demographic.

We need large-print paperback books. That's a good start. Here are a few more suggestions for products geared toward aging boomers:

- TVs with extra-loud sound so everybody sounds like Chris Matthews.

- Extra-large oat bran so you can find it in your bowl.

- Cars with magnifying-glass windshields so aging motorists can read road signs.

- Toilets that fold out into beds so a man has a place to sleep during all those nightly visits to the bathroom.

Be Strong, Fellow Boomers!
Stan Jantz

If you've ever driven down a highway making great time, only to hit a construction zone where you had to slow to a crawl in order to negotiate a rough patch of asphalt, then you know what it's like to be an aging baby boomer. The vehicle still works, but the ride isn't as smooth, and you certainly aren't moving as fast as you once were.

Don't get me wrong. I love being a boomer, and I wouldn't want to be anything else. I even love the name *boomer*. If ever there were a great description for a particular segment of the general population, this is it. Think about it. Other demographic monikers, such as *buster* (someone born between 1965 and 1983) or *mosaic* (someone born between 1984 and 2002) have somewhat negative connotations. Who wants to be a bust? Not me. And what's up with *mosaic*? It's confusing. *Boomer*

has none of this negative baggage. A boomer is confident and optimistic.

Nonetheless, I am enough of a realist to admit that confidence and optimism will carry you only so far, especially when you begin to encounter some construction zones in the highway of life. This reality became painfully clear to me recently when I had appointments with four different doctors and several medical labs in the span of less than two weeks. Keep in mind that there was nothing really wrong with me. It just so happened that my primary care physician wanted to follow up on some "irregularities" he had uncovered, and so he referred me to two different specialists. At the same time, I was due for my annual dental and eye exams.

As I ran from one appointment to another, I felt like a little boat caught in a big medical "perfect storm." I was tossed back and forth from one office to another. I was poked, prodded, and pricked every which way. I gave blood like I have never given blood, and I didn't have so much as a Twinkie to show for it. After a while, whenever I saw someone in a white lab coat, I automatically asked if they wanted me to give them a specimen. To add insult to injury, as I navigated my way through various doctors' offices and labs, I noticed that every medical professional was younger than I was. By at least ten years.

After a while, I detected a pattern in the way the doctors treated me. They would smile at me the way I smile at my mother and say encouraging things like, "You sure look good for your age." Are you kidding me? I look good *for my age*? Talk about hitting a rough patch of asphalt! That's not what you want to hear, unless you're ninety-five and living in a retirement home.

What's the use? I might as well admit it. As a baby boomer, I'm

no youngster. The harsh reality is that some of us boomers have now reached the age when we can begin to receive Social Security benefits. I can claim to still be a few years away from sixty-two, the age of the oldest boomers and the earliest age a person can begin drawing government checks for no other reason than being old. But the road I'm on isn't getting any smoother. And the vehicle I'm riding in—this body that's served me faithfully for so many years—isn't getting any younger.

But I'm not giving up. I'm a boomer, not a quitter! Confidence and optimism are my strengths. Never mind that at my age, these qualities are largely built on self-perception. From my perspective—the one that really counts—I'm still in the prime of my physical life. In my mind I look good, because in my

As long as I can still see my feet and there aren't too many hairs in my sink in the morning, I'm a happy camper.

mind I'm still thirty-five. As long as I can still see my feet and there aren't too many hairs in my sink in the morning, I'm a happy camper.

It also helps that my wife is a co-conspirator. As long as she willingly and lovingly participates in my little fantasy, I can get through the construction zones of life with flying colors. I don't like it when a doctor tells me I look good for my age, but when my wife tells me, I feel like a million bucks. Of course, I have to do my part to maintain the illusion. Whenever she looks at me with that sparkle in her eye and says, "I don't know anyone your age who looks as good as you do," I smile and quickly turn away

so I don't see her eye roll or crossed fingers. I also avoid looking in mirrors for prolonged periods.

So be strong, fellow boomers! Don't let those whipper-snapper health care professionals get you down. The next time a doctor half your age comments on how good you look for someone at your advanced stage of life, draw upon your reservoir of boomer confidence and optimism and tell yourself how good you look for someone at *any* age. And whatever you do, avoid looking in mirrors for prolonged periods.

Atten-shun!
Bill Cosby

All the failures of memory that can plague you, such as losing your car at a mall or losing your glasses on your forehead or losing the reason you entered a room, are minor when compared to the most embarrassing trick your mind can play: forgetting what you have been talking about. After scientists find a cure for the common cold, they will have to move on to a greater medical challenge: why a man my age clearly remembers events of thirty years ago but not what he said in the last thirty seconds. It is perhaps the most demoralizing moment that a middle-age man can know, even worse than learning that his twenty-six-year-old son is about to move back into the house or that his high school sweetheart has applied for membership in the Gray Panthers.

The moment happens to you like this. You and another friend in his fifties are sitting together, perhaps at a party where none of the younger people will talk to you because you still read books,

or perhaps in the waiting room of a doctor who specializes in the treatment of people who have begun to click. You have started talking to this man about a subject in which you always have been deeply interested: the history of hot chocolate. You can see that your friend is listening with attention as you spellbindingly reveal how the ancient South Americans invented hot chocolate

for an après-sacrifice: they would toss a fellow tribesman into a volcano and then relax with a nice hot cup. Not only are you being fascinating, but you are also building to a major medical point: that hot chocolate is the safest drug and should be given to babies before they develop a yen for something else.

You are trying to return to your train of thought and discover that you can't even find the station.

You are merrily spinning these unforgettable thoughts, while your friend is responding with continuous support: "Oh yes, Bill, absolutely . . . A point well taken, and I'm taking it well . . . you've a winged tongue there, man . . . for sure, Bill, for sure . . ."

But suddenly another person approaches you and says, "Would either of you gentlemen like some coffee?"

"No, thank you," you reply.

"No coffee for me," says your friend.

"Some tea or prune juice, perhaps?"

"No, thanks."

"None for me."

"Perhaps a mint or a Tootsie Roll?"

"No, nothing for me either."

"No, nothing, thanks."

"Right, nothing for me either."

And then you speak the chilling words, "Now where was I?"

You are trying to return to your train of thought and discover that you can't even find the station. And neither can your *friend,* who has been listening with such attention.

I have helplessly watched my mind shift into neutral on both sides of this grand embarrassment: as both the derailed storyteller and the lost listener. If you're the listener, you say to yourself, *He must think I haven't been listening, but I really have. I love stories about . . . about . . . about . . . whatever he was saying.*

And if you're the storyteller, your distress is even more painful, because your thoughts had been organized and you had been building to a point. You know many pointless stories, but this did not happen to be one. And so, seized by a mental power failure, the storyteller doubles back desperately in his memory, but he still cannot find the train of thought, which is running on a holiday schedule.

This is the general style of going blank one on one. If, however, the storyteller has been talking to more than one listener when he goes blank, then he has a chance to take a poll to reveal the subject he has been talking about.

"Listen, folks," he says, hoping that he is still concealing his dismay, "I never like to repeat myself, so please tell me if any of you has heard this story I was telling about . . . about . . ."

And hopefully he waits for someone to play *Password* with him.

But no one is able to play. At last, his mounting frustration makes him shed his subtlety and he says with a casual air, "By the

way, does anyone here happen to remember what I was talking about?"

"I'm afraid I don't," one listener will reply. "It happened too recently. But ask me about the night we put the donkey in the dean's office to celebrate Kennedy's election. Or ask me about the Battle of Gettysburg. Eighteen sixty-three is like yesterday to me."

"I can't remember it either," another listener will say, "but it was certainly memorable."

"Wait a minute now . . . it's coming to me," a third person will say. "Yes, here it *comes*. Chalk . . . chalk . . . You were talking about the history of *chalk*."

The lesson for us middle-agers in this piteous tale is clear: we cannot start a monologue leading to any kind of punch line or point unless we are in an environment where no interruptions are possible. The good environments for storytelling, like the confessional, you can figure out for yourself; but even in the ideal environment, people with sometime memories like mine should still tell only the shortest possible stories.

"Knock, knock," I said to my wife last night as we settled down to some sophisticated after-dinner talk.

"Who's there?" she replied, and I quickly moved my story to its sparkling conclusion.

If, however, my "Knock, knock" had been followed by a phone call from one of my children requesting money by Federal Express, the story would have been no easier to remember than my story of why those old South Americans got acne.

No matter what the length of your discourse happens to be, it is wise to carry a pencil and pad; and then, when someone

interrupts, you can say "Just a second" and write down exactly where you stopped. Of course, some people need more than a pad. Some people need cue cards.

The only good thing about the decline of my memory is that it has brought me closer to my mother, for she and I now forget everything at the same time. When I was younger, I used to look at my mother impatiently and think, *Lord, can't she remember anything?* But now that we go blank simultaneously, I look at her and think, *Is she supposed to say "Knock, knock" or am I?*

Hello Hello?

Forget It
Patsy Clairmont

I am the type of person who can walk from one room to another and not know why I've gone there. I know I had a reason when I began my trek, but I lost it on the way. Sometimes I try backing up in hopes it might come to me.

My family can usually tell this is the problem by the bewildered look on my face. Walking in reverse also seems to be a giveaway. Sometimes they try to help, and other times they just let me wander aimlessly, figuring I'll wise up or wear out.

I try to blame this forgetfulness on age. But those who have known me for years remind me that my wires have never all been touching, although turning forty has seemed to loosen a few more.

I read in an article that after we turn forty, one thousand brain cells die each day. But according to the writer, it doesn't matter because we have millions . . . or was that billions? Anyway, lots of them. My problem is, the cells I've been losing were filled with

valuable information I meant to retain—like where I'm going, how old I am, the names of family members, etc.

Names. Isn't it embarrassing when you know you know, but you draw a blank? I realize that our names are important to us, and we don't want to be forgotten. That's why I think name tags should be mandatory. They should be pinned on us at birth and removed after the funeral. Think of all the awkward moments that could alleviate.

The guy, oh, what's-his-name, who sang "I Left My Heart in San Francisco," doesn't know how lucky he is. I left my bifocals in Indiana, my alarm clock in Ohio, my Bible on an airplane heading for Texas, my slip in Colorado, and heaven only knows where my watch is . . . probably with my sunglasses and keys.

I think name tags should be mandatory. They should be pinned on us at birth and removed after the funeral.

Have you ever been digging through a drawer when all of a sudden you realize you don't know what you're looking for? If anyone is watching me, I just keep digging. I've found a lot of lost items that way.

It's disconcerting for me to dial the phone, and by the time the call connects, to find that my mind has

disconnected—I've forgotten whom I'm calling. Sometimes I hang up until I remember. Other times I listen, in hopes I'll recognize the voice. Occasionally I've been brave and confessed to the anonymous party that I can't remember whom I dialed and hope they'll claim me.

The point I'm trying to make is . . . is . . .

Bye, Bye, Miscellaneous Pie
Bill Gray

I live in fear of my own heart.

It's not a consuming thing. I don't think about it every morning when I wake up or every night just before I shut my systems down.

But it's there, palpable and palpitating, in my chest.

Throughout my childhood, my teen years, and my twenties, I assumed that the physical ailments that claimed my father's and grandfather's generations would have no effect on me. The young always think they're bulletproof.

It turns out that being bulletproof and looking good in tights are just two of the things I don't have in common with Superman.

Like many middle-age guys, the first time I learned my cholesterol number was too high, I was scared straight.

Oatmeal replaced the donuts. Lunch got lighter, and so did I. "Bippity-boppity-boo!" The afternoon candy bar turned into an apple!

As my cholesterol number fell, my fervor dropped off a bit with it. Surely one cookie at work wouldn't hurt. Or two. What was I supposed to do when I was out to dinner, somebody else was buying, and the peach cobbler looked so good? Could I turn down the pork chop my mother had so lovingly fried just for me?

After a while, oatmeal just gets to be so, well, oatmealy.

But then it would come, like a life preserver tossed from a passing ship: a cheap cholesterol screening.

The results would yank me back to reality the way a slap does for a panicky guy in a gangster film. My bad cholesterol would again be bad, my good cholesterol would be not so good, and it would be just the goose I needed to become obsessive about my diet again.

That is the cycle I've followed ever since. My theory is that all the ups and downs will even out into a pretty healthy diet.

Of course, the twin mantra of all soldiers in the war on cholesterol includes not only diet but also exercise.

I hit the bricks early on. They hit back.

My first experience with jogging came in my mid-twenties. I was out singing folk songs in a bar one night and ran out of breath on a fast song. Next day, I laced up bad shoes and went to a park where a one-mile course was laid out.

I have no idea what the far end of that course looks like.

At about the third jog, I began panting like fat Elvis live in Hawaii, and little lightning bolts of pain shot through my side.

My calves bawled, and each flat-footed thud sent a shockwave straight up to my teeth.

Jogging became like playing piano—just another thing that looked easy when other people did it. Just another thing I tried briefly before giving up.

Ten years later, after being kicked in the back pockets with that cholesterol number, I tried again. I still wheezed. I still ached. But I kept going. There would be no marathons in my future, but I worked up to a respectable couple of miles a day.

Exercise helped the cholesterol number fall. My spirits rose. It didn't last.

I had become a reader.

Normally, I think reading is a good thing. We encourage reading around my house.

The newspapers and magazines I read in those days featured all sorts of experts offering all sorts of advice on keeping that wicked cholesterol number down and putting heart disease in its place, which was not in my chest.

I read, I obeyed, I bored my friends with details and mini-sermons.

Then one day I read the awful word "genetics."

Heart disease, it turns out, has as much to do with heredity as it does with diet or exercise. Or more. Or not as much. It all depends on which expert you read.

I read them all and believed the worst.

My father had his first major heart attack in his forties. He died way too soon, in his early sixties, from a combination of cancer, diabetes, and heart disease.

Gulp.

So I live in fear of my own heart because it may be the heart of my father.

After reading the stuff about genetics, I could have just surrendered, hung up the jogging shoes, and ordered a big mess of chili fries, I suppose. But I didn't.

If I can't control heredity, I've decided to work a little harder at controlling the other stuff. I may just be kidding myself that it will do any good against a genetic predisposition, but, if that's the case, I have myself snookered.

That's why I'm at my company's fitness center most days, even though being there reminds me of stalling halfway up the rope in junior high gym.

"I will not lie down. I will not go quietly."

It's why I regularly humiliate myself in front of guys who have no gray hairs, who can probably do fifty push-ups without breaking a sweat, and who can pee whenever they feel like it.

It's why two lines from a song often go through my head while I work out. The song is not even one I particularly like, but the lines have become a motto.

It's a song off the *End of the Innocence* album by Don Henley, which does have good songs on it, including one of my favorites, "New York Minute." But my two workout lines are from one of the lesser tunes.

"I will not lie down. I will not go quietly."

They inspire me, even though I know they are just a less-poetic version of Dylan Thomas's "Rage, rage against the dying of the light. Do not go gentle into that good night."

It's still Don's two lines that come to mind when the treadmill seems to be going faster than it did last time I ran on it, or the weights seem to have gained weight since I last lifted them.

I will not go quietly.

There are too many things I still want to get done to play aces and eights at this stage of the game.

I want to travel with my wife after we both are retired. I want to watch my son graduate from college. I want to figure out all the words to "Green River." I want to sing "Yellow Submarine" to my grandchild.

Get thee behind me, genetics!

I will not lie down.

Popular Sports Adjusted for the Woman over Forty

Martha Bolton

Skydiving

Same as regular skydiving, only the jump involves floating back up to the plane at least once mid-jump to make sure you didn't forget something.

Figure Skating

Not only can an over-forty woman do this as well as a woman half her age, but she can also do it while carrying a purse!

Bowling

Many women over forty participate in this sport—not for the exercise—for the roomy shoes. Nothing handles puffy feet better than a good pair of bowling shoes.

Soccer

By the time a woman gets to forty years of age, she's encountered enough difficult people to give her a good selection from which

to choose a face to paint on the soccer ball. Once she's narrowed it down to the final one, she can kick the likeness to her heart's content.

NASCAR

Women can drive fast, too. Even the over-forty woman. The only difference is, for the over-forty NASCAR races, drivers are required to stay in the slow lane with their left turn signal on. The winner is the first to find a Waffle House along the speedway.

(Skin) Tag Football

Similar to regular tag football, with one small exception: I'm not saying what the players have to pull on to score a "tackle," but this sport has already put four thousand dermatologists out of business.

Boomer Baseball

Baseball with just one small tweak in the rules: any hairpieces or loose body parts that fly off the runner and land on home plate before she gets there herself still count as a point.

Boomer Basketball

Like regular basketball, only when a boomer gets called out for excessive dribbling, the ref usually calls for a mop.

Boomer Skiing

Nothing is quite as beautiful as watching a boomer make her way down a snow-covered slope, twisting to the right, curving to the left, doing a perfect double flip and ultimately coming to rest at the bottom of the hill. If done on purpose, that's even better.

Chapter 8

Great Goobers! We Have Grandchildren
(Grandchildren)

The Virgin

A ten-year-old, under the tutelage of her grandmother, was becoming quite knowledgeable about the Bible. Then one day she floored her grandmother by asking, "Which virgin was the mother of Jesus—the Virgin Mary or the King James Virgin?"

They're Out to Rule the World

Martha Bolton

The kids are taking over. I'm not talking about all the doctors, policemen, politicians, and attorneys who seem to be getting younger and younger each year. I'm talking about children. Real children. More specifically, toddlers. They could be your nieces and nephews, your grandchildren, your neighbors' kids, or in some cases, even your own children. And sure, they seem innocent enough sitting there in their cribs or on the floor, playing quietly with their toys, but it's all a ruse. They have an agenda, they're committed, and they've been outsmarting us for years. Everything they do is to advance their plan to take over the world, and it's high time someone blew their cover.

First, I'm not sure how they did it, but somehow these little rugrats have managed to take control of our television sets. Instead of watching our favorite news programs or the History Channel, we find ourselves caving in to their desires and watch-

ing SpongeBob and Jimmy Neutron for hours on end. Granted, we do get involved in the programs, and sometimes even catch ourselves laughing out loud, but has anyone played their theme songs backward to see if they're sending subliminal messages to the adult world?

"You will let me play ball in your house."

"You will take me to Chuck E. Cheese's."

"You will give me an advance on my inheritance."

"You will let me braid your hair in tiny little braids and paint your toenails fluorescent pink."

Who knows what kind of adult brainwashing is going on during these seemingly innocent children's shows?

Phase two apparently happened while many of us middle-agers were taking naps. These innocent-looking children somehow

"Sure, Gramps, as soon as you reveal the password to your safety deposit box."

convinced pharmaceutical companies of the need for our medicine bottles to come with childproof caps. Caps, I might add, that only *children* can open. Now on the surface, child-proofing medicine bottles probably sounded like a great idea, and I do not doubt for a minute that the staff at the FDA had plenty of reputable data to convince the agency to jump on board with the seemingly beneficial plan. But the FDA wasn't looking into the future to see where this action would take us as a society.

"I need my heart medication, Joey," Grandpa says. "Can you come over here and get this blasted thing open for me?"

"Sure, Gramps, as soon as you reveal the password to your safety deposit box."

These children are the same ones who also hide our glasses, car keys, wallets, and *TV Guide*, and then merely giggle, clam up, or speak some kind of gibberish when we try to interrogate them about the missing items.

"Where are my keys, Bobby?"

"Ahgagoga."

"Come on, boy, tell Nana where you put them."

"Dimofogu."

Their resistance to these inquisitions would impress military experts worldwide. Both the FBI and CIA have tried to decipher their secret code, but it's unbreakable.

We're headed for trouble, people.

And who is it that gets the power seat at the dinner table? The high chair? (See, even the name sounds commanding.) Who is responsible for that incessant pounding on the metal trays that would make even the toughest grandparent shout out every password to every account he's ever owned? These toddlers, that's who.

Remember the good ol' days when children used to be at the mercy of adults when it came to their mobility? They either rode in a stroller or we carried them. That, too, has changed. These days, kids have their own battery-operated cars to putt around in. They're eighteen months old, and they already know how to drive. What's worse, we're probably the ones they persuaded to buy these vehicles for them.

Which brings us to their incredible business sense. These youngsters are nothing short of financial geniuses. Think about it. They come to our houses selling candy for their schools and

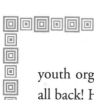
youth organizations, then they return on Halloween and take it all back! Has anyone done the math on this?

I'm telling you, world, their hostile takeover has been planned right under our noses and we've been too blinded by their cuteness to see it. They've been holding high-level security meetings in sandboxes all over the globe. Sure, it all looks like innocent play to us, but it isn't. It's their version of Camp David. Why do you think there's always one child who holds that ear-piercing, high-pitched scream? You think it's a tantrum? I used to think that, too.

These toddlers have their own cell phones, computers, play-houses, and miniature emergency vehicles. What do they need us big people for? They've got almost everything required to run the world on their own.

The most amazing thing about this is how these little ones have managed to get us to run their publicity campaigns for them, and we've been doing it pro bono.

"You wanna see some pictures of the most beautiful grand-child on earth?"

"You think she's beautiful, wait 'til you see my grandbaby!"

All things considered, maybe we're just getting what we deserve. These little ones have been outsmarting us for years, manipulating us with their cute smiles and endearing hugs, while we've merely sat by and allowed it all to happen.

But it's not too late. No matter how cute they are, we cannot continue to roll over and let these kids take over. We can't bury our heads and pretend we don't know what they're up to. It's time we let them know once and for all who's in charge here! It's time we . . .

Sorry. I had more to say, but a two-year-old in my doctor's waiting room just took my glasses and won't give them back, so I can't see my laptop keys. And so the conspiracy continues . . .

What My Youngest Grandchild Taught Me

Nancy Hoag

They say it isn't easy growing old, but that's not actually true. Growing older happens by itself, whether we help it along or not. It's the futile attempt to seem more with it than we are. That's what wears us out, and futile is the word. My five-year-old grandchild helped me see that, funny little person that she is.

We were riding in the backseat of her mother's SUV; Delaney was gabbing away, relating tales I'd already heard, but I was there because she'd pleaded, "Mom-Mom, *please* sit with me!" When her Papa and I visit, she meets us at the door, bag packed and begging to sleep in my room. She brings her crayons and we color together, read, and play. This morning, though, her mom and I wanted to gab, so I hadn't been paying all that much attention.

Until, that is, the smallest voice in the car caught me off guard with, "My *other* grandma can do *every*thing!"

Her other grandma? Surely she didn't mean—!

For reasons admittedly childish, the "other" felt like a bad taste in my mouth. But, shifting in my seat, I reminded myself Delaney was only a child, so I needed to cool it. I smiled and calmly asked, "What *every*thing can she do?"

"Well . . . she can dance and do gymnastics and swim—"

I don't dance, it plays havoc with my bunions! You couldn't pay me to do gymnastics; I have a bad back! And swim? Puleese!

"Does she write books?" I asked, unable to stifle the juvenile tone, but the "*Every*" had set me off. Furthermore, writing books is the one thing someone as old as dirt can do! "Well?" I asked, feigning composure.

My granddaughter tossed me the look that meant, "So, what does writing *books* have to do with anything?"

This child was smart: that twinkle told me she knew exactly what she'd said. She'd been taking teasing lessons from her teenage sister's friends, and heard daily how she couldn't do this or that.

"Well," Delaney was saying now, "no, she doesn't but—"

"Well," I sang, "*I* can."

"No you can't." Arms wrapped across her chest, my grandchild strained forward in her car seat to show me her bossiest face.

I began to smooth my denims, hoping I looked like the groovier writer and grandma. "Well, I *can*," I said, unwilling to let this child believe someone else could be awesome when I could only be old.

"Unh, unh," Delaney whooped.

This time, her mother turned around with, "Mom-Mom does too write books!"

Three cheers for my daughter; I would leave her something extra in my will.

"I'll show you one when we get home," Lisa said. "It's a book, all right, with her picture on the back."

Hooray for Delaney's mother! She understood that I didn't need to hear what I'd just heard, and writing was a sport, of sorts. "So . . ." I lifted my chin at the child who had, until now, been my best friend. "What do you think about that?" *Go ahead, act like a kid; she needs to understand you aren't totally worthless.* "Well?" I asked again.

My granddaughter leaned all the way sideways to meet me nose-to-nose, and then, acting like the teen she longed to be, she threw her hands up to her face and sang, "Actually, I don't think you'd look that *good* on the back of a book!"

"Not *that* good?" I croaked as my mouth dropped . . . and I began to laugh.

I was still laughing when my daughter turned and said, "Delaney, that was rude! Mom, why are you laughing? She insulted you!"

She'd been taking teasing lessons from her teenage sister's friends, and heard daily how she couldn't do this or that.

"I know," I said, grabbing a tissue to wipe mascara from my face, re-membering how that morning a visiting teen had teased Delaney about the "cute little" boots she had chosen, and then Delaney's sister had announced that she was too young to go with them anywhere, and she needed to fix her hair . . . and now she was looking to see if I'd be saying the same . . . only I wasn't and I could not.

"Because we're in the same boat," I whispered, as Delaney pulled a package of Sweet Tarts from her kitten purse and held one out for me. "Love you," I said, touching her flushed cheek. "She helps me keep things in perspective, so I don't take life too seriously," I added, leaning now toward my daughter.

It wasn't much fun growing older, but neither did Delaney enjoy being the youngest, shortest person in her world. "Together, though, we make a real pair," I said, popping a candy into my mouth and exchanging grins with the grandchild who, when I reacted to her yanking my chain, had experienced the measure of success she'd been needing . . . and who would one day grow beyond the limitations of her age.

"And so will I," I laughed. "So will I."

Brain Freeze
Gwendolyn Mitchell Diaz

I was performing one of my favorite grandmotherly duties—spoiling my grandchildren rotten! This particular time I was feeding Kaelyn and Jeremiah ice cream on a hot summer day. It was a special treat, and they were enjoying it thoroughly.

Suddenly, Jeremiah scrunched up his little four-year-old face and started pounding his forehead with the palm of his hand.

"Jeremiah, what are you doing?" I wanted to know.

"I've got brain freeze!" he wailed.

It was obvious that he had suffered from this malady before, since he knew exactly how to identify it.

I smiled on the inside, and jumped up to pour him a glass of tap water hoping that it would ease the freeze. Then he asked a question that stumped me.

"Why did God make brain freeze when it hurts so bad?" he queried with his own four-year-old grammar.

"Well, ummmm . . . well," I stammered in response.

How on earth do you explain the whole problem of pain and suffering to a four-year-old?

Do you go back to the Garden of Eden and explain how perfect things were before Adam and Eve took a bite out of the forbidden fruit? (You don't dare identify it as an apple when you're talking to a four-year-old, or he might never eat another one again.)

And if you do start your answer with an explanation of Adam and Eve in the perfect paradise, then the next time your grandchild comes over, he's going to want you to take him to the Garden of Eden to play. And he's going to want to know, "Is it kind of like Disney World?"

As I sat there stumped, I realized that Jeremiah wasn't the only one with brain freeze.

And when you explain that it didn't have roller coasters or musical shows, he'll wonder why on earth God wasted time building it—and does it have a lake with jet skis?

I realized that I could try a different approach and explain how God sometimes uses pain and suffering to help us grow. But then Jeremiah would want to stay little for the rest of his life so that his head wouldn't hurt.

All my possible answers were triggering red flags. However, I reasoned that if Jeremiah was old enough to blame God for the pain that was taking place in his life, it was probably my responsibility to offer him a decent explanation.

As I sat there stumped, I realized that Jeremiah wasn't the only

one with brain freeze. I was suffering a terrible case of it myself! Even though I had answered this question dozens of times at high school retreats and before youth groups, and wrestled through it with college students at a forum, and written a book that included a chapter with a carefully delineated explanation of the issue, I couldn't come up with a four-year-old explanation to save my life!

Finally, as he stared at me, waiting for my response, I replied, "Hey, that's a great question, Jeremiah. We'll have to ask God when we get to heaven."

"Okay," he replied. Just like that—case closed!

He scraped the bottom of his bowl, took one last sip of water, and jumped down from his seat. He ran out into the yard to play with his sister, his brain sufficiently thawed. Apparently, the best answers are the simple ones!

Chapter 9

Rest and Riches
(Retirement)

Speaking of Retirement

"Retirement at sixty-five is ridiculous. When I was sixty-five I still had pimples."

GEORGE BURNS

"One of the problems of retirement is that it gives you more time to read about the problems of retirement."

ANONYMOUS

Bob's Retirement

Author Unknown

Dear Friends,

It is important for men to remember that as women grow older it becomes harder for them to maintain the same quality of housekeeping as they did when they were younger. When men notice this, they should try not to yell. Let me relate how I handle the situation.

When I got laid off from my consulting job and took early retirement in March, it became necessary for Nadine to get a full-time job, both for the extra income and for the health benefits that we need. It was shortly after she started working that I noticed she was beginning to show her age.

I usually get home from fishing or hunting about the same time she gets home from work. Although she knows how hungry I am, she almost always says that she has to rest for half

an hour or so before she starts supper. I try not to yell; instead I tell her to take her time and just wake me when she finally does get supper on the table. She used to do the dishes as soon as we finished eating. Now it is not unusual for them to sit on the table for several hours after supper. I do what I can by reminding her several times each evening that they aren't cleaning themselves. I know she appreciates this, as it does seem to help her get them done before she goes to bed. Now

that she is older, she seems to get tired much more quickly. Our washer and dryer are in the basement. Sometimes

 she says she just can't make another

If I have a really good day of fishing, it allows her to gut and scale the fish at a more leisurely pace.

trip down those steps. I don't make a big issue of this. As long as she finishes the laundry the next evening, I am willing to overlook it.

Not only that, but unless I need something ironed to wear to the Monday lodge meeting, or to Wednesday's or Saturday's poker club, or to Tuesday's or Thursday's bowling, or something like that, I will tell her to wait until the next evening to do the ironing. This gives her a little more time to take care of some odds and ends, like shampooing the dog, vacuuming, or dusting.

Also, if I have a really good day of fishing, it allows her to gut and scale the fish at a more leisurely pace.

Nadine is starting to complain a little occasionally. For example, she will say that it is difficult for her to find time to pay the monthly bills during her lunch hour. In spite of her complaining, I continue to try to offer encouragement. I tell

her to stretch it out over two, or even three days. That way she won't have to rush so much. I also remind her that missing lunch altogether now and then wouldn't hurt her any, if you know what I mean.

When doing simple jobs, she seems to think she needs more rest periods. Recently she had to take a break when she was only half finished mowing the yard. I try not to embarrass her when she needs these little extra rest breaks. I tell her to fix herself a nice, big, cold glass of freshly squeezed lemonade and just sit for a while. I tell her that as long as she is making one for herself, she may as well make one for me and take her break by the hammock so she can talk with me until I fall asleep.

I know that I probably look like a saint in the way I support Nadine on a daily basis. I'm not saying that the ability to show this much consideration is easy. Many men will find it difficult. Some will find it impossible. No one knows better than I do how frustrating women can become as they get older. However, guys, even if you yell at your wife just a little less often because of this article, I will consider writing it worthwhile.

Bob.

Bob's funeral was on Saturday, April 25.
Nadine was acquitted Monday, April 27.

Things That Go Beep in the Night
Colleen Frye

When my husband and I hit our mid-forties, we eschewed navel piercings, tattoos, extramarital flings, or an expedition to Everest in favor of new running shoes and sports watches (safer alternatives than the other choices, we thought). After years of languishing on the couch, eating popcorn and watching TV after the kids went to bed, we figured we better catch up with our figures if we had any hope of catching up with our now teenagers. But it turned out that catching up with technology was the biggest challenge.

Granted, it had been a long time since either one of us had done any running, but running shoes still look basically the same. Of course, they come in a lot more colors, and there are high-tech designs for every type of runner—like overpronaters or underpronaters (although I didn't see any for procrastinators). And granted, some of the lacing constructs look like they were derived

from the *Book of Knots,* but you don't need an owner's manual to use them: You put them on, tie them up, and go.

The sports watches, we found out, were a lot more like our son's MP3 player than our old Timexes—they weren't designed for ordinary adult mortals who feel like rocket scientists when we successfully download a song. We discovered that while we were eating popcorn, engineers were designing these watches to do a lot more than tell you the time after you've dripped sweat all over them. Now they can time your run, time your laps, time your splits, time your cookies in the oven, monitor your heart rate, set multiple alarms, measure the barometric pressure, ascertain the altitude, and gauge the temperature—all in multiple time zones. The sports watch can also wake you up, remind you of what you almost forgot, beep you, vibrate you, glow in the dark, tell you if you're heading north or south, and make dinner reservations—oops, sorry, that last feature is for my PalmPilot, which I still haven't figured out, either.

Really, we only needed to know if we ran slower than the day before. However, we gamely got out the directions, which were printed in at least seven different languages, plus Morse code, and, using a magnifying glass to see the buttons, somehow managed to set the date and time. I dreaded daylight saving time, though, as it was only by sheer luck that we managed to push the right buttons in the right sequence. So far so good.

Until that night, when a strange beeping wakened me about three A.M. I didn't recognize the sound, and it eventually stopped. My husband slept through it. Several nights went by like that until I figured out that the problem was the alarm on one of the watches—we must've set it somehow. We pulled out the directions and started pressing more buttons. We couldn't even find the alarm function, never mind shut it off.

"I'm going to try the German directions," said my husband. "I may have a better shot at it."

Despite his best Deutsch, the beeping arrived on schedule that night.

"We're going to have to give it the Barney treatment," I whispered to my husband in the dark.

Anyone who has had a child in the last decade is familiar with the sugary-sweet purple dinosaur who says "You're super-dee-duper" and romps on PBS with a group of grade-schoolers who, strangely, never seem to age.

The "Barney treatment" was born one night several years ago—also around three A.M.—when the battery-operated Barney my son was sleeping with malfunctioned and started saying, "You're super-dee-duper" over and over and over again.

"We're going to have to give it the Barney treatment."

I stumbled through the dark to my son's room with the intent of yanking the batteries, but it required a screwdriver. So I shook it—throttled it, really—and it was still telling me I was super-dee-duper. I ran down the stairs and hurled it into the cellar. No more super-dee-duper.

I didn't hurl those watches, but I did carry them down to the cellar. I placed them near the boxed-up DVD player that insisted upon playing in "random mode" and for some reason disrupted our cable TV. From now on, I told my husband as I crawled back in bed, the watches live in the basement when we're done running. Problem solved.

"You're super-dee-duper," my husband whispered as he dropped back off to sleep.

Something to Think About!

Author Unknown
Adapted by Rebecca Currington

Like most boomers, I've been giving serious thought to what will happen to me during my golden years. Long single, I'm going to have to depend on others for my care. So imagine my delight when I discovered the answer while cruising through the Caribbean aboard a Princess cruise liner.

At dinner on the first night, my friend and I noticed an elderly woman sitting alone in the main dining room. The staff, including the ship's captain, were quite attentive. Always curious, I asked our waiter who the woman was, expecting to be told she was an heiress or Bill Gates's mother. Instead, I was told that the mystery woman had been on board for the last four cruises.

As we left the dining room one evening, I stopped by her table. We chatted until I could get up my nerve to inquire. "I understand you're on your fourth consecutive cruise," I said with a smile.

"Yes, that's true," she replied, smiling back. I wasn't budging without more.

"Could I ask why?" I said, expecting to be put in my place.

"Well . . . ," she quickly answered, "It's better than a nursing home—and cheaper too!"

She went on to explain to me that a nursing home costs about 200 dollars per day. The cost aboard a Princess cruise? About 145 dollars per day (with senior-citizen discounts). Add 10 dollars per day for gratuities, and you're still ahead! Make that 15 dollars and the staff will be begging to treat you like a queen!

And consider these amenities:

1. Ten great meals a day (the last one at midnight even has an ice sculpture!). If you can't make it to one of the great dining rooms, you can order room service and have breakfast in bed every day of the week.

2. Free toothpaste, razors, soap, and shampoo.

3. TV repaired, lightbulbs changed, mattresses replaced. Energetic young men and women will fix anything and everything and apologize for your inconvenience.

4. Free sheets and towels every day without asking.

5. Free housekeeping—friendly folks come in each day to clean the bathroom, make the bed, and vacuum.

6. Three swimming pools, a workout room, free washers and dryers, all without maintenance fees or additional costs.

7. Floor shows and other entertainment available every night.

8. The opportunity to meet new and interesting people every seven to fourteen days.

9. Treated like a customer, rather than a patient. "Yes, ma'am!" "Of course, ma'am!" "Will there be anything else, ma'am?"

10. The opportunity to see Asia, the South Pacific, the Caribbean, Alaska, New Zealand, Australia, and Italy (just for starters).

No sir, there won't be a nursing home in my future. My retirement plan is all about a Princess cruise ship! Yippee!

Retirement Community

Martha Bolton

I have to say that the thought of moving to a retirement community has never really interested me. I haven't reached retirement age yet, but for years I've been convinced that to feel youthful and vital, one needs to be surrounded by young people.

But I think I might need to back up and rethink that for a moment.

After having lived next door to teenagers who seem to have no direction in their lives, throwing parties while their parents are away, playing loud music till all hours of the night, walking down the street with their boom boxes blaring, and constantly revving their car engines, a retirement community doesn't seem so bad anymore.

Also, in a retirement community you usually don't have people trying to "find themselves." Most of the residents are

pretty comfortable with who they are. By the time you reach retirement age, you don't have to prove anything to anyone. You're comfortable in your skin. It might not be as tight a fit as it once was, but you're comfortable.

Retirement communities don't have to deal with gangs, either. You won't see "AARP" spray-painted on the sides of buildings, and no one will be standing on the corner peddling B_{12} shots.

Another advantage to living in a retirement community is that older citizens usually realize the importance of showing good manners and consideration for one's neighbors. Their wild parties are over by nine o'clock, and the only mess they make is when someone pours too much Epsom salt in the Jacuzzi.

The only mess they make is when someone pours too much Epsom salt in the Jacuzzi.

I have to admit the advertisements for some of these retirement communities today are pretty enticing. They depict golf courses, waterfalls, gardens, community centers

with monthly guest speakers covering a variety of interesting topics, holiday parties, and much more. Some of these places offer restaurant facilities and shopping, as well as a post office, a drug store, and other business offices. They are their own villages. Some even offer gyms and personal trainers.

And the people pictured in the brochures don't even look old anymore. They look youthful and vibrant, and they seem to be having the time of their lives enjoying all the activities and spending their children's inheritance.

So on second thought, when my husband and I get ready to retire, maybe we'll look into moving to a retirement community. We like peace and quiet. We like mannerly neighbors. And we're usually in bed by nine o'clock, anyway. As for the Epsom-salt Jacuzzi? I guess it's like they say. You don't know if you'll like it unless you try.

Chapter 10

Tales of the Open Road
(Adventure)

Senior Driving

As a senior citizen was driving down the freeway, his car phone rang. Answering, he heard his wife's voice urgently warning him, "Gary, I just heard on the news that there's a car going the wrong way on Interstate 77. Please be careful!"

Gary answered, "It's not just one; it's *hundreds* of them!"

Larry Walters
Robert Fulghum

Let me tell you about Larry Walters, my hero. Walters is a truck driver, thirty-three years old. He is sitting in his lawn chair in his backyard, wishing he could fly. For as long as he could remember, he wanted to go *up*. To be able to just rise right up in the air and see for a long way. The time, money, education, and opportunity to be a pilot were not his. Hang gliding was too dangerous, and any good place for gliding was too far away. So he spent a lot of summer afternoons sitting in his backyard, in his ordinary old aluminum lawn chair—the kind with the webbing and rivets. Just like the one you've got in your backyard.

The next chapter in this story is carried by the newspapers and television. There's old Larry Walters up in the air over Los Angeles. Flying at last. Really getting UP there. He's still

sitting in his aluminum lawn chair, but it's hooked on to forty-five helium-filled surplus weather balloons. Larry has a parachute on a CB radio, a six-pack of beer, some peanut butter and jelly sandwiches, and a BB gun, to pop some of the balloons to come down. And instead of being just a couple of hundred feet over his neighborhood, he shot up eleven thousand feet, right through the approach corridor to the Los Angeles International Airport.

The Larry Walterses of the earth soar upward, knowing anything is possible.

Walters is a taciturn man. When asked by the press why he did it, he said: "You can't just sit there." When asked if he was scared, he answered: "Wonderfully so." When asked if he would do it again, he said: "Nope." And, asked if he was glad that he did it, he grinned from ear to ear and said: "Oh, yes."

The human race sits in its chair. On the one hand is the message that says there's nothing left to do. And the Larry Walterses of the earth are busy tying balloons to their chairs, directed by dreams and imagination to do their thing.

The human race sits in its chair. On the one hand is the message that the human situation is hopeless. And the Larry Walterses of the earth soar upward, knowing anything is possible, sending back the message from eleven thousand feet: "I did it, I really did it. I'm FLYING!"

It's the spirit here that counts. The time may be long, the vehicle may be strange or unexpected. But if the dream is held close

to the heart, and imagination is applied to what there is close at hand, everything is still possible.

But wait! Some cynic from the edge of the crowd insists that human beings still *can't really* fly. Not like birds, anyway. True. But somewhere in some little garage, some maniac with a gleam in his eye is scarfing vitamins and mineral supplements, and practicing flapping his arms faster and faster.

Safe Travel

Margot Starbuck

A lot of folks I know pray for safe travel when they fly. A confident, seasoned traveler, I begin my early morning cross-country journey without giving the Heavenly One a second thought.

As the world's teeming masses kick their luggage through a roped-off labyrinth of despair, I proudly saunter up to the airline's easy kiosk check-in. Swatting like a toddler at anything on the screen that resembles a button, I decide that *easy* is in the eye of the beholder.

The eyes of the other passengers burn a hole in the back of my stylish travel outfit. I can tell they're thinking, "She looks like she'd be so *good* at easy kiosk check-in." For a split second, I wistfully recall when the only button an air traveler could be trusted to push at will was the round silver *recline* button on the airplane seat's armrest—and then only when authorized by the flight crew. After I refresh the check-in welcome screen for the seventh

time, a disgruntled passenger waves an employee over to help me. Miraculously, the employee's techno-magic checks me in.

At my next stop I have big plans to outwit transportation officials who are waiting to confiscate liquids from unsuspecting travelers. In an act of radical civil disobedience I uncap my $1.39 liter of water, throw my head back, and chug it down. Stashing the empty in my backpack, I run my sleeve across my wet face and eyeball the transit official as if to say, "You want a piece o' this?"

I have big plans to outwit transportation officials who are waiting to confiscate liquids from unsuspecting travelers.

You know that old line about pride going before a fall? The transit official radios ahead to instruct the pilot of my flight to linger on the runway just as my seatbelt-strapped bladder reaches maximum capacity. That's going to hurt.

Next stop, X-ray security checkpoint. Like so many other line-bound travelers, I am left with nothing to do but dream up illicit ways to smuggle something through. I'm actually pretty proud of a few of them.

The procedure feels strangely like what happens in a discount clothing retailer's dressing room. Keep an eye on my valuables. Take off purse, shoes, and coat. For a split second I worry that I'll just keep going. "Don't-take-off-your-shirt-don't-take-off-your-shirt," I repeat under my breath.

When a guard instructs me to take off my cute corduroy jacket, I lobby, "Oh, it's not a *coat*. It's part of my *outfit*."

"Take it off."

"But, my T-shirt's too small because—"

"We've got a CODE RED!" he barks into his walkie-talkie.

"I'm doing it! Go ahead and take a look at these fat rolls, mister!"

I won't lie and say it was my finest moment. Truth be told, though, I do feel a little safer knowing that any potential terrorists with body-image issues might think twice before attacking the land of the free.

No one's told me what I'm supposed to carry through the laser arch. I know that I should *not* carry scissors, razor blades, or automatic weapons, but what about my purse? Ticket? Driver's license? Honestly, I feel more panicky about the arch guy with the beepy wand than I do about slim terrorists.

In the end I cling to my boarding pass and driver's license. I hold them both in the air as if to beg, "Don't shoot!"

Glowering at my license, the agent hisses with disgust, "Don't need it."

Scooting back into my shoes, I glance at my boarding pass. Whether they call it A-2 or A-28, there is no doubt in my mind that the gate on my boarding pass will be the *last* gate in the terminal.

It is.

On the way, I traipse past a string of odd retail establishments.

Brooks Brothers is having a sale. My pulse quickens, "It's my *last chance* to shop for the next four hours! What do I *need* from Brooks Brothers?"

That's so wrong.

I console myself with the knowledge that if I truly need to make an impulse purchase while I'm flying, there is always the $4,500 inflatable lake trampoline in the Sky Mall catalog.

Reaching the gate, my luck finally turns when I score a front-row spot in front of CNN airport news. After eating a snack from my purse, I want to throw away my trash but fear I'll lose the great seat. A quick glance around the gate area confirms that everyone else with a good view of the TV is *also* clutching trash.

By the fifth viewing of a looping reel that features the Mashed Potato Wrestling Champion of the Universe and bikini baristas, it becomes evident that the seat isn't *that* great.

I make a quick dash for the restroom.

Leaving a self-flushing toilet unflushed (not my fault!) and performing a complicated choreography of dance moves in front of the no-touch faucet, I still can't get the water on. I do the same futile routine for the no-touch soap and paper towels. Strangely, I find myself pining for the germ-infested handles, knobs, and levers of yore. Ahhh—those were the good old days.

By the time I board, I am completely exhausted. Even if I did smuggle through the dangerously sharpened carrot stick I had conjured up, I'd be too tired to use it.

Squeezing into my incredibly narrow seat—when did they shrink those?—and banging my knees against the seat tray in front of me, I suddenly realize that there's more to travel prayers than asking God to keep my plane from falling out of the sky. Maybe inhabiting a prayerful spirit on my travel day wouldn't have been *such* a bad idea after all.

You Are What You Drive
Robert Fulghum

Transportation is much the topic of the day. You've noticed. Our devotion to the car is worshipful. Eric Verne called it the cocktail-party pastime game "General Motors."

Despite what you hear, it's not really a matter of economics. It's an image issue. In America, you are what you drive. Go out in the garage and look. There you are.

Well, my old hoopy has joined the cripples on the edge of the herd. And a new vehicle (image) is in order.

The silver-gray Mercedes with glove-leather everything really felt like me. The bank did not really think it felt like me to them. The shiny black BMW motorcycle with sidecar kind of felt like me. My wife did not think it felt like her—especially the sidecar part. The Land Rover with gun rack and shooting top felt like me. But there are so few game-covered veldts around town now. The VW Rabbit is *Consumer Reports'* choice, but a Rabbit I am

just not. If they had named it the VW Walrus or the VW Water Buffalo, I might go for it. The Chrysler Coupe de Coupes de Coupes won't do, either. Who wants to be an anachronism?

One of my students suggested putting all my money into drugs. Stay home and take all the trips you want. But that's not me—you don't bring back groceries from those trips.

It's clear that what would be fashionably hip is a fine piece of engineering—something that's luxurious yet practical, useful, and economical. Like a Porsche pickup truck that runs on Kleenex. Silver-gray, of course.

What I really want from transportation is not an image but a feeling.

I remember riding home on a summer's eve in the back of an ancient Ford pickup, with two eight-year-old cousins for company and my uncle Roscoe at the wheel. We'd been swimming and were sitting on the inner tubes for comfort, and had a couple of old quilts and an elderly dog wrapped close for warmth. We were eating chocolate cookies and drinking sweet milk out of a mason jar, and singing our lungs out with unending verses of "Ninety-nine Bottles of Beer on the Wall." With stars and moon and God o'erhead and sweet dreams at the end of the journey home.

Now *that's* transportation. The way I like to travel. And that's me. If you hear of a dealer, let me know.

Contributors

Marti Attoun is a weekly humor columnist for her hometown newspaper, the *Joplin* [Mo.] *Globe*, is a contributing editor for *American Profile* magazine, and has published hundreds of articles in regional and national publications, including *Reader's Digest, Redbook, Christian Science Monitor, Family Circle, Ladies' Home Journal* and *Good Housekeeping.*

Charlene Ann Baumbich is a self-professed (and rightly so) wild child of God. Whether her stories bloom straight out of her crazed life or her zany imagination, she can't wait to share them. Subscribe to the TwinkleGram (www.twinklegram.com) to keep up with her latest adventures, or visit www.dontmissyourlife.com.

Zarette Beard lives in Colorado with her husband, Thomas, the love of her life; their witty teenage son, Sabian; Sophie, the

toy poodle; and Louis, the Bouvier. She is an honors graduate from Regis University and has published her work in *Guideposts*, *Focus on the Family*, and many other publications. She is well traveled, collects antiques, and makes Thanksgiving dinner four or five times a year.

Martha Bolton is a former staff writer for Bob Hope, a two-time Angel Award recipient, an Emmy nominee, and the author of more than thirty books, including *Didn't My Skin Used to Fit?* and the "Official" Book Series.

Polly D. Boyette is the author of *Life Is a Buffet, So Save Room for Dessert*, a collection of humorous short stories about her life and family experiences. She was born and raised in Virginia, where she still lives today. Polly loves to laugh and share her gift of storytelling.

Patsy Clairmont is one of the founding speakers of Women of Faith and the author of twenty books. Her latest releases are *Dancing Bones . . . Living Lively in the Valley* and *I Second That Emotion . . . Untangling Zany Feelings.*

Bill Cosby is a highly successful comedian beloved by American audiences for his stand-up routines, *Fat Albert* cartoon series, commercials, and his blockbuster sitcom, *The Cosby Show*. A teacher at heart, Cosby received his doctorate in education in 1977.

Rebecca Currington, who served as compiler, is the founder and president of Snapdragon Group℠, where she marshals a

workforce of 450 freelance writers, editors, compilers, reviewers, and proofreaders. Together they typically produce between fifty and sixty scripts per year for Christian publishers around the country. Read more about it at www.snapdragongroup.com.

Gwendolyn Mitchell Diaz grew up with her parents on the mission field before taking on the task of raising four active sons. Her humorous insights on marriage and motherhood are recorded in several books, including *The Adventures of Mighty Mom.*

Brad Dickson was a monologue staff writer for *The Tonight Show with Jay Leno* for fourteen years. Before that he was a working screenwriter, placing several screenplays with motion picture companies. Since leaving *The Tonight Show,* he has been writing recurring humor columns for the *Los Angeles Times, L.A. Daily News,* and the *Jewish World Review* website. He has also developed a groundbreaking pilot for a major television network.

Colleen Frye is a humor writer who has had stories published in *Working Mother, First for Women, Equal Times,* and on iParenting.com. She lives in Massachusetts with her husband and two children, who are still trying to teach her how to use all the features on her new cell phone.

Robert Fulghum has made his living as a ditchdigger, cowboy, IBM salesman, folksinger, parish minister, bartender, newspaper columnist, and philosopher. His books, *All I Really Need to Know I Learned in Kindergarten, It Was on Fire When I Lay Down on It, Maybe (Maybe Not), Uh-Oh, From Beginning to End,* and *True Love,* have sold more than fifteen million copies in twenty-seven languages in ninety-three countries. He has four children and seven grandchildren. He lives with his wife, a family physician, on a houseboat in Seattle, Washington.

Bill Gray is a humor writer, musician, and baby boomer who has made his way to fifty-something with a soundtrack playing in his mind. It's the sound of a dozen garage bands; the sound of revolution meeting middle age; and always, always the sound of four guys from Liverpool whom he has never met. When he isn't writing humor cards for Hallmark, Bill loves being with his wife, Carolyn, and son, Aaron, at their home in Shawnee, Kansas, where sometimes he plays guitar, sometimes he plays drums, and sometimes he just plays.

Dixon Hearne, a Louisiana native, teaches and writes in southern California. His stories can be found in *Mature Living, The Louisiana Review, Cream City Review,* and elsewhere. He has received several writing awards, and his new short story collection, *Tethered Hearts,* is in review at a university press.

Nancy Hoag, who currently lives in Montana, is an award-winning teacher, speaker, and the author of more than 900 articles, devotions, and columns that have appeared in nearly 160 publications. She has added four nonfiction books to her credits, including *The Fingerprints of God: Seeing His Hand in the Unexpected,* Baker Books/Revell.

Elece Hollis, an accomplished writer, lives in northeastern Oklahoma with her husband, Ron. She spends her days homeschooling the three youngest of their seven children.

Stan Jantz is a businessman and author who has cowritten sixty books, including the international bestseller, *God Is in the Small Stuff.* Stan and his writing partner, Bruce Bickel, are the founders of ConversantLife.com, a content and social media hub that encourages conversations about faith.

Vicki J. Kuyper has been a freelance writer for the last twenty years, writing everything from inspirational books to training videos to sheep pun calendars. Vicki resides in Phoenix, Arizona, and her sister, Cindy, lives in Colorado Springs. Despite the miles and the years, they remain close at heart.

Sue Fagalde Lick, a former newspaper editor, has published countless freelance articles, short stories and poems, plus three books. In addition to writing, she sings and plays guitar and piano, leading her church choir and performing at local venues, preferably in loose garments made in such wonderful colors that nobody worries about what size they are. She'd really like to know why humans are the only animals who aren't encouraged to fill out in their mature years. Sue and her husband, Fred, live in South Beach, Oregon. Visit her website at www.suelick.com.

Karen Scalf Linamen is a motivational and inspirational speaker, and the author of fourteen books. Her titles include *Just Hand Over the Chocolate and No One Will Get Hurt,* and *Due to Rising Energy Costs, the Light at the End of the Tunnel Has Been Turned Off.* Karen lives in Colorado and writes for a living. Contact her at www.karenlinamen.com.

Marnie Macauley is the author of the advice column, "Ask Sadie," and has written more than twenty books and calendars, including *Yiddishe Mamas: The Truth About the Jewish Mother,* and the series, *A Little Joy, A Little Oy.* Her scripts for *As the World Turns* have garnered Emmy and Writers Guild nominations. A frequent media presence, she also starred in a pilot for the Discovery networks. She is in *Who's Who in America, 2007.*

Cherie Rayburn is a freelance writer and the president of The Creative Word. She lives in Colorado Springs, Colorado.

Carol McAdoo Rehme discovered her childhood toys in an antique mart, giggled—and wrote about it. A freelance editor, author, and ghostwriter, she publishes prolifically in the inspirational market and has coauthored five gift books. Carol recently coauthored *Chicken Soup for the Empty Nester's Soul* (2008). Contact her at carol@rehme.com; www.rehme.com.

Anita Renfroe is an author, comedian, and YouTube phe-*mom*-enon. After posting her "Total Momsense" video on YouTube, Anita became an overnight viral Internet sensation (more than 15 million views and still counting). This mother of three has appeared on ABC's *Good Morning America,* CBS's *The Early Show, Dr. Phil,* and Fox News Channel's *Fox and Friends.* She also performed at the 2007 Women of Faith Conferences. Watch for her new DVD release, *It's Probably Just My Thyroid.*

Randy Richardson is an attorney for the Social Security Administration's disability appeals branch. At night and during

lunch breaks, he serves as president of the Chicago Writers Association and works on his second novel while a four-year-old tugs on his legs.

Jeff Sawyer has published humor in a variety of newspapers and written jokes for *The Late Show with David Letterman*. He is a creative director for an international clothing company located in the Midwest, and writes www.sawyerspeaks.wordpress.com, a blog that is usually funny on purpose.

Margot Starbuck is a writer and speaker living in Durham, North Carolina, with her husband, Peter, and their three children. Every time Margot flies with her family she says a happy prayer that her children no longer wear diapers. Learn more about Margot's writing and speaking ministry at www.MargotStarbuck.com.

Source Notes

Chapter 1: Play It Again, Sam

"Remember When . . ." Author Unknown.

"Therapeutic Theme Songs" by Karen Scalf Linamen. Used by permission of the author.

"10 Memorable Pairs of Pants" by Bill Gray. Story taken from *50-Something: Fond and Funny Reflections on Midlife* by Bill Gray, copyright © 2005 by Hallmark Books, a division of Hallmark Cards Inc. Used by permission of Hallmark Licensing, Inc. All rights reserved.

"Turn On, Tune In, Drop Everything" by Bill Gray. Story taken from *50-Something: Fond and Funny Reflections on Midlife* by Bill Gray, copyright © 2005 by Hallmark Books, a division of Hallmark Cards Inc. Used by permission of Hallmark Licensing, Inc. All rights reserved.

"Time Travel in the Sixties" by Vicki J. Kuyper. Used by permission of the author.

"Angus MacGyver and Other Long-lost Loves" by Karen Scalf Linamen. Used by permission of the author.

"Speed Reader on Board" by Marti Attoun. Used by permission of the author.

"Fifty-nine-and-three-quarters" by Dixon Hearne. Used by permission of the author.

"Solving Problems, Retro-Style" by Karen Scalf Linamen. Used by permission of the author.

"2-GOOD 2-BE 4-GOTTEN" by Bill Gray. Story taken from *50-Something: Fond and Funny Reflections on Midlife* by Bill Gray, copyright © 2005 by Hallmark Books, a division of Hallmark Cards Inc. Used by permission of Hallmark Licensing, Inc. All rights reserved.

Chapter 2: That Person in the Mirror Can't Be Me!

"Twenty Perks of Being Over 50 . . ." Author Unknown.

"You're as Young as You're Ever Gonna Be" by Anita Renfroe. Story taken from *The Purse-Driven Life* by Anita Renfroe, copyright © 2005. Used by permission of NavPress, Colorado Springs, Colorado (www.navpress.com). All rights reserved.

"Runner's High" by Zarette Beard. Used by permission of the author.

"Mountain Boomer" by Jeff Sawyer. Used by permission of the author.

"Hooked on the Ladies' Hair Journals" by Marti Attoun. Used by permission of the author.

"Color-coded" by Patsy Clairmont. Used by permission of the author.

"Moose in a Noose" by Sue Fagalde Lick. Used by permission of the author.

"PWSD (Pre-watersport Stress Disorder)" by Karen Linamen. Used by permission of the author.

"Exercising Our Prerogative?" by Martha Bolton. Excerpt taken from *Cooking with Hot Flashes*, copyright 2004 by Bethany House, a division of Baker Publishing Group. Used by permission.

Chapter 3: For Better or For Worse

"What Is This?" Author Unknown.

"Do You Know This Man—'Cause I Certainly Don't!" by Gwendolyn Mitchell Diaz. Used by permission of the author.

"Mixed Messages" by Patsy Clairmont. Used by permission of the author.

"Taking Tea Down Under" by Elece Hollis. Used by permission of the author.

"Lois . . . What's Her Name?" by Marnie Macauley. Used by permission of the author.

Chapter 4: The Perilous View from the Top

"Does It Work?" Author Unknown.

"View from the Web" by Robert Fulghum. Story taken from *All I Really Need to Know I Learned in Kindergarten* by Robert L. Fulghum, copyright © 1986, 1988 by Robert L. Fulghum. Used by permission of Villard Books, a division of Random House, Inc.

"Looking for Love on the Wrong Planet" by Cherie Rayburn. Used by permission of the author.

"Things We Still Don't Know After All These Years" by Martha Bolton. Excerpt taken from *Race You to the Fountain of Youth*, copyright 2007. Published by Howard Books, a division

of Simon & Schuster, Inc., 1230 Avenue of the Americas, New York, NY 10020. Used by permission.

"No Batteries" by Robert Fulghum. Story taken from *All I Really Need to Know I Learned in Kindergarten* by Robert L. Fulghum, copyright © 1986, 1988 by Robert L. Fulghum. Used by permission of Villard Books, a division of Random House, Inc.

Chapter 5: Who Are These People?

"A Letter to Bubba" Author Unknown.

"Be It Ever So Rent Free" by Bill Cosby. Story taken from *Fatherhood* by Bill Cosby, copyright © 1986 by William H. Cosby Jr. Used by permission of Doubleday, a division of Random House, Inc.

"Buy the Book" by Carol McAdoo Rehme. Used by permission of the author.

"Mother-of-the-Bride Blues" by Elece Hollis. Used by permission of the author.

"Recharging an Old Battery" by Randy Richardson. Used by permission of the author.

"Hail to Thee, Bankruptcy" by Bill Cosby. Story taken from *Fatherhood* by Bill Cosby, copyright © 1986 by William H. Cosby Jr. Used by permission of Doubleday, a division of Random House, Inc.

Chapter 6: Who's Watching Mom and Dad?

"Divorcing After 45 Years" Author Unknown.

"Living in Life's Twilight Zone" by Elece Hollis. Used by permission of the author.

"Say What?" by Polly D. Boyette. Used by permission of the author.

"I'm Alive!" by Charlene Ann Baumbich. Used by permission of the author.

Chapter 7: Embracing Bingo!

"A Tip for Remembering" by Al Sanders. Taken from *I'm Trying to Number My Days, but I Keep Losing Count,* copyright © 1998. Published by WaterBrook Press.

"It's My Birthday" by Bill Gray. Story taken from *50-Something: Fond and Funny Reflections on Midlife* by Bill Gray, copyright © 2005 by Hallmark Books, a division of Hallmark Cards Inc. Used by permission of Hallmark Licensing, Inc. All rights reserved.

"Please Excuse My Purchase. I was Insane" by Marti Attoun. Used by permission of the author.

"Large-print Books" by Brad Dickson. Excerpt taken from *Race You to the Fountain of Youth,* copyright 2007. Published by Howard Books, a division of Simon & Schuster, Inc., 1230 Avenue of the Americas, New York, NY 10020. Used by permission.

"Be Strong, Fellow Boomers!" by Stan Jantz. Used by permission of the author.

"Atten-shun!" by Bill Cosby. Story taken from *Time Flies* by Bill Cosby, copyright © 1987 by William H. Cosby, Jr. Used by permission of Doubleday, a division of Random House, Inc.

"Forget It" by Patsy Clairmont. Used by permission of the author.

"Bye, Bye, Miscellaneous Pie" by Bill Gray. Story taken from *50-Something: Fond and Funny Reflections on Midlife* by Bill Gray, copyright © 2005 by Hallmark Books, a division of Hallmark

Cards Inc. Used by permission of Hallmark Licensing, Inc. All rights reserved.

"Popular Sports Adjusted for the Woman over Forty" by Martha Bolton. Excerpt taken from *Race You to the Fountain of Youth*, copyright 2007. Published by Howard Books, a division of Simon & Schuster, Inc., 1230 Avenue of the Americas, New York, NY 10020. Used by permission.

Chapter 8: Great Goobers! We Have Grandchildren

"The Virgin" Author Unknown.

"They're Out to Rule the World" by Martha Bolton. Excerpt taken from *Cooking with Hot Flashes*, copyright 2004 by Bethany House, a division of Baker Publishing Group, Grand Rapids. Used by permission.

"What My Youngest Grandchild Taught Me" by Nancy Hoag. Used by permission of the author.

"Brain Freeze" by Gwendolyn Mitchell Diaz. Used by permission of the author.

Chapter 9: Rest and Riches

"Speaking of Retirement" Author Unknown.

"Bob's Retirement." Author Unknown. Adapted by Rebecca Currington.

"Things that Go Beep in the Night" by Colleen Frye. Used by permission of the author.

"Something to Think About!" Author Unknown. Adapted by Rebecca Currington.

"Retirement Community" by Martha Bolton. Excerpt taken from *Growing Your Own Turtleneck*, 2005 by Bethany House, a division of Baker Publishing Group. Used by permission.

Chapter 10: Tales of the Open Road

"Senior Driving" Author Unknown.

"Larry Walters" by Robert Fulghum. Story taken from *All I Really Need to Know I Learned in Kindergarten* by Robert L. Fulghum, copyright © 1986, 1988 by Robert L. Fulghum. Used by permission of Villard Books, a division of Random House, Inc.

"Safe Travel" by Margot Starbuck. Used by permission of the author.

"You Are What You Drive" by Robert Fulghum. Story taken from *All I Really Need to Know I Learned in Kindergarten* by Robert L. Fulghum, copyright © 1986, 1988 by Robert L. Fulghum. Used by permission of Villard Books, a division of Random House, Inc.